MEN-AT-ARMS SE

EDITOR: MARTIN WIND_ROW

Central American Wars 1959-89

Text by CARLOS CABALLERO JURADO
and
NIGEL THOMAS

Colour plates by SIMON McCOUAIG

OSPREY PUBLISHING LONDON

Published in 1990 by
Osprey Publishing Ltd
59 Grosvenor Street, London W1X 9DA
© Copyright 1990 Osprey Publishing Ltd

British Library Cataloguing in Publication Data

Thomas, Nigel, *1946–*
    Central American wars, 1959–89.
    1. Central America. Military equipment history
    I. Title   II. Series
    623'.09728

    ISBN 0-85045-945-1

Filmset in Great Britain
Printed through Bookbuilders Ltd, Hong Kong

Authors' Note and Acknowledgements
This survey of Central America and the Caribbean
would not have been possible without the kindness and
unstinting assistance of a number of correspondents
and friends, many over many years. Nigel Thomas
would like to thank Peter Abbott (always a tower of
strength); Jean-Yves Goffi; Dr. Marc Landry; M.
Albert Mendez; Julio A. Montes; Frank Steff;
Lt. Cdr.(ret.) W. Maitland Thornton OBE; and his
family, Heather, Alexander and Dominick. Carlos
Caballero acknowledges gratefully Vicente Talon,
editor of 'Defensa' magazine, for his help in providing
a great deal of information, documentation and
photographs. Any corrections and additional
information would be welcomed from readers.

    As with any recent or current conflict, the authors
are naturally aware that the Central American
situation arouses understandably strong political
opinions among many different groups. Every effort
has been made to avoid seeming to make political
judgements in a text which is intended solely as an
objective record of facts.

Artist's Note
Readers may care to note that the original paintings
from which the colour plates in this book were
prepared are available for private sale. All
reproduction copyright whatsoever is retained by the
publisher. All enquiries should be addressed to:
    Simon McCouaig
    4 Yeoman's Close
    Stoke Bishop
    Bristol BS9 1DH

The publishers regret that they can enter into no
correspondence upon this matter.

Central American Wars 1959-89

Introduction

In the conflicts covered in this text we will not encounter huge tank battles, savage aerial combats nor bold naval operations. We are concerned here with less spectacular guerrilla wars, where most fatalities are caused by brutal acts of terrorism or reprisal rather than by conventional warfare. However, it would be a serious error to underestimate the importance of these disputes in Central America and the Caribbean, sometimes called 'the North American Mediterranean'. In fact many analysts refer to the region as 'the United States's second Vietnam', and predict that it will become 'the Middle East of the Year 2000'.

An examination of these conflicts suggests two types of problems. In almost all these countries there are serious divisions in society, combined with the pressure of large foreign interests, notably those of the United States. These factors encourage a desire for social and economic change within the country. Secondly, in most of these countries there exist powerful interests which seek to prevent peaceful political evolution. Furthermore, the armed forces have usually tried to prevent a democratic solution to these problems by coups d'état followed by military dictatorships.

Western countries have not adopted a uniform policy towards this situation. European states tend to prefer a diplomatic solution linked to a programme of economic development; but the United States, with important strategic and economic interests in the region, has usually opted for a military solution. Since Fidel Castro's victory in Cuba in January 1959 the United States has been concerned that any change of government in a Central American country should not usher in a similar Soviet-backed communist regime; and to prevent this it has developed a range of responses, from direct military intervention, through support

General Francisco Tabernilla, Army Chief of Staff, with Contralmirante Julio Rodriguez Calderon, Navy Chief of Staff, in Batista's Armed Forces, 1958. Tabernilla wears the standard Cuban light tan service dress.

of local armies, to diplomatic isolation and economic blockade. Part of this strategy has been the training of tens of thousands of Latin-American soldiers in anti-guerrilla warfare techniques at the 'School of the Americas', functioning in the Panama Canal Zone since 1946.

For the first time in their history, Latin-American states have recently established a diplomatic framework to head off the danger of future United States military interventions in the region. In 1983, when the US invasion of Grenada seemed to presage the imminent invasion of Sandinista Nicaragua, the states of Mexico, Venezuela, Colombia and Panama set up the 'Contadora Group', later joined by four more South American countries. This diplomatic pressure group has sought to prevent the escalation of conflicts, and encouraged peaceful solutions, as in the First and Second Esquipulas Accords.

Influenced by the 'Vietnam syndrome', the United States has adopted a strategy to deal with the low-intensity conflicts in the region. In accordance with the 'domino theory', it works to prevent the installation of revolutionary regimes which might trigger off a chain-reaction in neighbouring countries.

Although all the wars under study have origins predating Castro's victory in 1959 (dating from at least 1926, in the case of Nicaragua), we concentrate here on their evolution since then. It was to take 20 years, until July 1979, for a left-wing movement to emulate Castro's achievement, with the establishment, not yet consolidated, of the Sandinista regime in Nicaragua, but the absence of victory by revolutionary forces does not mean that they have been eradicated. For the foreseeable future Central America and the Caribbean will remain a powder keg.

Cuba

Castro's victory in Cuba in 1959 opens our historical period. A charismatic leader, Fidel Castro Ruiz, a law student, was able, with a small force which never exceeded 3,000 guerrillas, to defeat Gen. Fulgencio Batista's *Ejercitó Constitucional* (Constitutional Army) with 38,000 soldiers and members of the *Guardia Rural*. His achievement contradicted the Marxist-Leninist thesis that

only a mass movement under a revolutionary workers' party could seize power, and this offered new channels of revolutionary possibilities.

Cuba, nominally independent on 10 December 1898 with the United States' defeat of Spain, the colonial occupier, was to become a virtual American colony. The United States, under the Platt Amendment of 12 June 1901, unhesitatingly intervened militarily in 1906, 1913, 1917 and 1933, ensuring that political power remained with pro-US politicians in spite of nationalist and left-wing opposition. From 5 September 1933 Batista, originally an army sergeant, effectively ran the country through a series of puppet presidents before finally becoming president himself in 1952.

Increasing opposition to his corrupt rule produced, on 26 July 1953, an attack by 111 armed men led by Castro on Moncada barracks, Santiago de Cuba, Oriente Province. The attempt failed and Castro fled to Mexico, establishing there the '26 July Movement'. On 2 December 1956 he and 82 men landed from the ship *Granma* on Las Coloradas beach in the Sierra Maestra, Oriente Province, a region of mountains and jungle, to initiate a guerrilla war which culminated in his

Castro gesticulates during his victory speech at Santa Clara, January 1959, after the capture of the town by 'Che' Guevara.

victorious entry into Havana on 8 January 1959.

Castro was defeated in his first clash with regular troops on 5 December 1956, but he regrouped with 500 recruits and new supplies. On 28 May 1957 he captured El Uvero barracks, an achievement commemorated as the foundation of his *Ejercitó Rebelde* (Rebel Army). In early 1958 Castro opened a second front in the Escombray Mountains, Las Villas Province. The United States suspended aid to Batista in March, alleging human rights violations; but in April a general strike called by anti-Batista factions failed.

Batista's army was organised, from west to east, into the 6th Rural Guard Regiment in Pinar del Rio Province; the Infantry Division under Gen. Rodriguez (1st 'Cuatro de Septiembre' and 2nd 'Diez de Marzo' inf. regts., tank regt., airborne, artillery and engineer bns.) and 5th Rural Guard in Havana; 4th Rural Guard in Matanzas; 3rd Rural Guard plus infantry bn., tank and artillery detachment in Las Villas; 2nd Rural Guard in Camagüey; and in Oriente, 7th Rural Guard with infantry bn. and tank detachment at Holguin, 1st Rural Guard plus two infantry bns., two tank and two artillery detachments at Santiago, infantry regt. plus tank and artillery detachments at Bayamo, and an infantry bn. plus tank and artillery detachments at Guantanamo.

In May Batista unleashed a general offensive, which ground to a halt in July, with Castro well established in all the provinces except Havana and Matanzas. In August 1958 the two best guerrilla commanders, Camilo Cienfuegos and the Argentinian Ernesto 'Che' Guevara, sent their columns racing towards Central Cuba from the west and east respectively, and on one occasion 200 guerrillas defeated 5,000 demoralised troops. Meanwhile other anti-Batista groups were joining Castro's forces. On 28 December 1958 Santa Clara, capital of Las Villas Province, fell, and on 1 January 1959 Batista fled Cuba.

The rebels, well led and motivated, had exploited opposition to Batista, and attracted sympathisers by humane treatment of the civil population. The army, with too many senior officers chosen for political loyalty, had lost heart. Disbanded in January 1959, it was initially replaced by the 'Revolutionary Militia' (1 May 1980 renamed 'Territorial Troop Militia'—MTT), and in mid-

The unit patch and tab of '2506 Brigade'—the Cuban exiles who fought and lost at Cochinos Bay ('Bay of Pigs') in April 1961.

1959 by the new *Fuerzas Armadas Revolucionarias* (Revolutionary Armed Forces), 25,000 strong, comprising Army, Navy and Air Force, backed by Militia regiments, Labour Youth Army and Civil Defence Force.

The Bay of Pigs

On 17 April 1961, 1,443 CIA-backed Cuban exiles in six 200-man 'battalions'—1st (Paratroop), 2nd (Infantry), 3rd (Armoured), 4th (Heavy Gun), 5th (Infantry), and 6th (Infantry), collectively called '2506 Brigade'—landed in the Bay of Pigs on the south coast of Central Cuba. They were confronted by a fierce counterattack by Castro's troops and militia, and on 19 April the surviving 1,200 exiles surrendered. Castro then signed a military alliance with the Soviet Union, which was to lead to the Cuban missile crisis of October 1962.

One of Castro's declared objectives was the exporting of revolution to Asia, Africa and Latin America, as proclaimed in the 1966 Tricontinental

2506 Brigade prisoners-of-war, some still wearing the brigade's camouflage field uniform, under the watchful eye of Castro's People's Militia, who helped defeat the invaders.

Conference in Havana. Revolutionary groups in Latin America sought to emulate the Cuban victory, and Castro was implicated in several attempts to establish guerrilla movements, the most famous being in Bolivia in 1967 under 'Che' Guevara. However, his prime concern was to defend Cuba against counter-revolutionary groups backed by the United States. The US government, for its part, sees the hand of Castro behind all left-wing movements in Central America, hence the Grenada invasion (see MAA 159). These suspicions are difficult to prove, but there is undeniably a large Cuban military presence overseas, from military missions in Algeria, Ghana, Guinea-Bissau, Somalia, Libya, Tanzania, Zambia, Syria and Afghanistan, to sizeable contingents in Angola (at its peak 50,000 soldiers, 8,000 civilians), Congo (500), Ethiopia 1978–84 (4,000), Mozambique (600), South Yemen (500) and Nicaragua (500 soldiers, 3,000 civilians).

Current forces

At present the Cuban Army has three armoured, three mechanised and 13 infantry divisions in Western Army (Pinar del Rio, Havana provinces)—one corps; Central Army (Matanzas, Las Villas)—one corps; Eastern Army (Camagüey, Oriente)—two corps; Isle of Youth (formerly Isle of Pines)—one infantry division. Each corps has three infantry divisions (three two-battalion regts.; artillery regt.; recce. bn.; services); and each Army HQ has one armoured division (one artillery, one mech., three tank regts.) and one mechanised division (one artillery, one armd. recce., one three-battalion tank, three two-battalion mech. regts., services). There are 26 independent AA regts. and SAM brigades, eight infantry regts., one Special Force Brigade (two bns.) and one Airborne Brigade. There is also a 12,000-strong Navy with a marine battalion; an 18,500-strong Air Force; 17,000 State Security troops (like Soviet KGB); 3,500 Frontier Guards; and in reserve, 1,200,000 Militia, 100,000 Labour Youth and 50,000 Civil Defence.

The long (three-year) military service period; efficient, well-trained armed forces; extensive combat experience in Africa and Asia; and a vigorous reserve force, make Cuba the greatest military power in the Caribbean after the United States. However, an analysis of its equipment—with few amphibious landing-craft or transport aircraft—suggests that the FAR is primarily a defensive force, permanently on alert for a US invasion.

Mexico

Despite its turbulent history, culminating in a revolution lasting from 1910 almost to 1930, Mexico, the northernmost country of Central America, has escaped the spiral of violence—military dictatorships, coups d'état, guerrilla warfare—endemic in the region. The peculiar Mexican political system, with the PRI (*Partido Revolucionario Institucional*—Institutional Revolutionary Party) as the only de facto political party, and the social system created by the revolution, have prevented the emergence of an effective rural guerrilla force (in spite of several abortive attempts in Guerrero State, 1967–74) or any sign of urban guerrillas. The decentralised Army and police forces have been able to stop any such activity at source.

Even so, Mexico's foreign policy is traditionally opposed to the United States (it has not forgotten two defeats by its northern neighbour in 1846–8 and 1916–17), and Mexico supports both politically and diplomatically Castro's Cuba, Sandinista Nicaragua and the Salvadorean guerrillas.

In 1981 Mexico announced an expansion programme for the armed forces, which had declined

The Mexican Minister of Defence, backed by other general and field officers. The black dress cap bears gold lace peak embroidery and chin strap, and a gold cap badge surmounted by silver rank stars and a green/white/red (outer) national cockade. The pale tan uniform shirt worn with a white undershirt has gold collar insignia, and black shoulder boards with silver stars, gold button, gold motif and gold lace. The national shoulder title is gold and maroon. In fact the Mexican Army uniform is impressive in its adherence to a continuous tradition of development, and by Latin-American standards is very restrained in its ornamentation. (ECPA)

The 23,000-strong Navy, geared for coastal defence, includes 3,800 Marines in one airborne brigade, one Presidential Guard bn., 13 groups and 32 security companies. The 6,500-strong Air Force (with a parachute brigade of 2,000) contains as a priority COIN and transport aircraft. Finally there are 300,000 reserves, and the paramilitary Rural Defence Corps (the famous *Rurales*) with 120,000 men on police duties under Military Zone commanders.

Guatemala

In the mid-1960s Guatemala looked set to become a second Cuba, and indeed has been in a state of virtual civil war for 30 years. In 1950 the then president, Col. Jacobo Arbenz Guzmán, carried

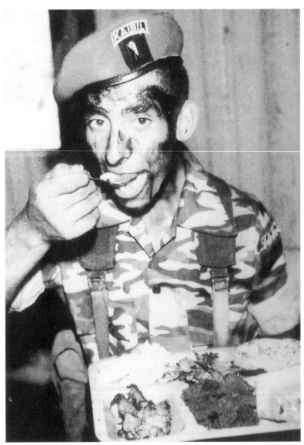

A Guatemalan Special Forces trooper proudly wears his red beret as he eats his last good meal before leaving on a jungle reconnaissance patrol. Note 'Kaibil' qualification tabs on beret and left shoulder. (Peter Abbott)

Troopers of the 2nd Dragoon Regiment, Mexican Cavalry, in field-parade dress with white parade neck-scarves, olive green uniforms, and cavalry sabres. (Vicente Talon)

in effectiveness through neglect, in order to promote itself as a regional power financed by huge oil revenues. The subsequent collapse in world oil prices brought serious financial problems which forced abandonment of the expansion, and so the Army remains relatively weak.

Current forces
The Mexican Army is basically organised for internal security. It has 134,500 men dispersed amongst 36 Military Zones in independent units—69 infantry battalions, 24 cavalry regiments (some motorised) and three artillery regiments. There are two infantry brigades (each with one armoured recce., one artillery, two infantry battalions) established 1968, in Mexico City; but the most important unit is the élite Presidential Guards Mechanised Brigade with HQ, I-III infantry bns., Assault Troops, artillery, transport, armoured recce. (two armoured car, one tank, two SPG companies) battalions, Mortar Group, logistics, engineer and medical companies.

This scene speaks volumes about the tension between the Central American soldier and the rural population: a Guatemalan farmer stands rigid with fear as he is interrogated by Army paratroopers searching for guerrillas. Note South Korean camouflage fatigues and Israeli helmet. (Vicente Talon)

out a series of social and political reforms which provoked an invasion in 1954 by groups of mercenaries organised by the CIA (who provided unmarked support aircraft) and supported by conservative political parties, the Church and part of the Army. Col. Carlos Castillo Armas was subsequently appointed president, but later in 1954 was faced with a rebellion by nationalistic Army cadets. On 13 November 1960 his successor, Gen. Ydigoras, faced another revolt, this time by nationalistic and left-wing sections of the Army; and many of the young officers implicated in these uprisings went on to establish the Guatemalan guerrilla groups. After Ydigoras came a series of military or militarily controlled governments, through fraudulent elections or coups d'état, until the free election of the Christian Democrat Vinicio Cerezo in 1985.

'Machismo' (exaggerated masculinity), always a powerful psychological force in Latin America, is particularly pronounced in the Guatemalan Special Forces; this sergeant wrestles playfully with a jungle python. (Peter Abbott)

Guatemalan infantrymen in field uniform, their features betraying their Indian origins. (Peter Abbott)

Araña Osorio, trained by 1,000 US Special Forces, carried out throughout 1966–7 ambitious operations to eradicate the FAR's *Frente Edgar Ibarra* from its stronghold in the Las Minas Mountains, Eastern Guatemala. The guerrillas turned their attention to the towns, achieving worldwide publicity by assassinating US diplomats. Even so, their effectiveness declined after 1970, when Araña, now president, unleashed a harsh campaign against them, with the full support of ultra-right-wing paramilitary groups.

The guerrilla war revived when Araña stood down in 1974, when new guerrilla groups were formed: the 'Guerrilla Army of the Poor' (EGP) in 1975, and the 'Armed People's Revolutionary Organization' (ORPA) in 1979. Both groups recruited mainly from the Guatemalan Indians, the most deprived social group in the country. The war against them has led to authenticated instances of massacres of Indians in those provinces where the guerrillas are strong—Quiché, Huehuetenango and San Marcos, Western Guatemala. These breaches of human rights led President Carter to suspend military aid in 1978, only for Israel to step in as the main source of aid.

The first guerrilla group, formed in 1962 in Izabal Province, Eastern Guatemala, by ex-Army officers, called itself the '13 November Movement'. Later it combined with various small extreme-left organisations choosing the armed struggle, as the 'Revolutionary Armed Forces' (FAR), which in 1963 conceived the over-ambitious plan of surrounding the capital, Guatemala City, and isolating it from the rest of the country. The Army, now expanded to 8,000, easily defeated them, but they managed to establish a new guerrilla splinter-group, the 'Edgar Ibarra Front'. The Army's success was compounded by political quarrels amongst the guerrillas, with the disaffected 'Guatemalan Workers' Party' (PGT) setting up its independent guerrilla units.

In 1966 these internal disputes were resolved and guerrilla numbers began to increase. Meanwhile the Guatemalan Army, under Col. Carlos

Guatemalan troops enter a village on a routine reconnaissance patrol against guerrillas; again, note South Korean 'wave' camouflage.

Members of a village Civil Defence Patrol in Guatemala, only their obsolete rifles indicating their military status. Most are Indians, led by a Spanish-speaking villager.

In 1982 the four guerrilla groups—FAR, PGT, EGP and ORPA—formed an alliance, the 'Guatemalan National Revolutionary Union' (URNG), to co-ordinate strategies. The same year yet another coup brought Gen. Efraín Ríos Montt to power, proclaiming a state of siege in order to 'finish the guerrillas once and for all'. He was succeeded, also through a coup, by Gen. Mejías who, in order to requalify for US aid, involved Guatemala increasingly in the anti-Sandinista political campaign, and moved towards greater democracy. This allowed President Cerezo to win power in January 1988 and, in February, to apply the 'Esquipulas Accords' which united Central American presidents in May 1984 and June 1987, and to begin negotiations with the URNG. A section of the Army wishing to continue the war against the guerrillas responded with an abortive coup. After losing more than 2,500 men (official Army figures; guerrilla estimates are much higher) in the civil war, the Army still wished to prevent peace negotiations. Today the 1,500 strong guerrillas are confined to remote areas whilst the Army receives increased aid from the U.S.A.

Current forces

Although Guatemala still has territorial claims on Belize—formerly a British colony, and since 21 September 1981 an independent Commonwealth state protected by a British Army and RAF garrison—the Guatemalan Army is not prepared for a conventional war, but is organised for counter-insurgency operations. It has expanded from 14,000 in 1980 to 38,000, dispersed throughout 19 Military Zones. There are 39 infantry, one Military Police and one engineer battalions, one armoured squadron, 18 field and two AA batteries, seven reconnaissance squadrons (with Israeli RBY-1 and US M8 armoured cars), 1st Paratroop Battalion (formed 1 January 1971) and the 'KAIBIL' Special Forces Group (two bns.). The last remnant of the former brigade organisation is the two-battalion Presidential Guard Brigade. There are few heavy weapons; most of the light weapons are Israeli.

The 1,500-strong Navy (including a 650-strong Marine Battalion of four companies) and the 700-strong Air Force are of minimal value. The Ríos Montt government organised a 'Civil Defence Patrol' (PDC) to defend villages against guerrilla incursions; though poorly trained, it is however 725,000 strong.

The guerrilla war has cost at least 20,000 lives (official figures), but it has lost the intensity of the 1960s when it was Central America's most serious conflict. Although weak, the guerrillas have not been eradicated in spite of Army methods— massive displacements of populations into 'model villages' guarded by the PDC; raids against refugee camps in Mexico; and civic action programmes, called 'Guns and Beans'—and their presence has diverted the Army from a more active rôle in Central American affairs.

El Salvador

This country, the smallest (only 8,124 square miles) and most densely populated in Central America, has suffered tremendous social upheavals for many years. In 1932 17,000–30,000 peasants were killed by the dictator Maximiliano Hernández Martínez's army after the 'Izalco Revolt', after which the communist leader Farabundo Marti was executed. In defending their sectional interests the ruling 'Fourteen Families' have relied on the support of the United States, which was reputedly involved in the coup d'état of January 1961. From 1961 to 1979 the 'National Conciliation Party' (controlled by the Salvadorean Army) dominated the political scene, forcing a growing extremism by opposition groups.

In 1969 El Salvador conducted the 'Football War' against Honduras. The origin of the dispute was 300,000 illegal Salvadorean immigrants in Honduras, and tension increased after two football matches in June 1969 had each resulted in visiting supporters being attacked by the local Honduran or Salvadorean population. On 12 July there were border clashes, and on the 14th the Salvadorean Army (peace-time strength 4,500 with three single-battalion infantry regiments, a mechanised cavalry, artillery and engineer battalion, expanded to 15,000 by mobilising 12 reserve infantry battalions) crossed into Honduras, occupying Nueva Ocotepeque (Northern Honduras) and El Amatillo and Nacaoné (Eastern Honduras). The 3,500-strong Honduran Army retaliated weakly, but its Air Force eventually achieved air superiority. On 18 July the Organisation of American States called a ceasefire, finally imposing economic sanctions on El Salvador after further localised fighting, and forcing it to withdraw from Honduran soil by 5 August. The war cost 3,000 dead and wounded, and intensified the hostile climate between the two countries.

This military adventure made Salvador's internal situation deteriorate, and now guerrilla groups emerged. In 1970 a splinter group of the Salvadorean Communist Party formed the 'Popular Liberation Forces—Farabundo Martí' (FPL-FM), building on experience gained in an attempted revolt in the 1960s. In 1972 the 'People's Revolutionary Army' (ERP) was established by left-wing Christian and Maoist groups; in 1975 the 'Armed Forces of National Resistance' (FARN or RN), an ERP splinter group, and the 'Revolutionary Party of Central American Workers' (PRTC). Finally, in 1979, came the 'Liberation Armed Forces' (FAL), the military wing of the Communist Party.

At present the FPL-FM, now called FMLN, with 2,600 guerrillas, and the ERP's 2,700 account for 80 per cent of the guerrilla strength, the other groups—FARN (600 guerrillas), FAL (500) and PRTC (250)—being much less significant. There are also three foreign guerrilla groups—*Alfaro Vive Carajo* (Ecuador), *Tupac Amaru* (Peru) and *Bandera*

A member of the Salvadorean National Guard's crack 'COPARA' rapid reaction anti-terrorist company poses with his Yugoslav M60 rifle-grenade launcher. (Julio A. Montes)

Roja (Venezuela)—operating in El Salvador. All groups are supported by political parties, trade unions and other national organisations.

1980 saw the guerrilla war escalating from acts of terrorism. The government stepped up the oppression and 'death squads'—secret assassination groups reputedly under extreme-right control—emerged. On 22 January an anti-government demonstration was put down with 200 dead or injured; and on 24 March Archbishop Romero, an outspoken critic of the government, the extreme right and the ruling oligarchy, was gunned down in cold blood. Now the entire left-wing opposition united in the 'Democratic Revolutionary Front' (FDR), composed of political parties, trade unions and other national organisations. In October 1980 the guerrillas combined as the 'Farabundo Martí National Liberation Front' (FMLN), allying with the FDR to co-ordinate political and diplomatic action, with the ambition of repeating the Sandinista victory in Nicaragua in July 1979.

The guerrillas divided their activity into four zones, covering El Salvador's 14 provinces, named after famous anti-government activists, and corre-

A Salvadorean armoured car crew relax before moving against guerrilla positions near Suchitoto, July 1981. The gunner (right) is reading the Spanish edition of *Reader's Digest*; his companion is the driver-observer. (Vicente Talon)

sponding to the Army's West, Central and East Military Zones:

'Feliciano Ama' (Western Front)—Santa Ana, Ahuachapan, Sonsonata Provinces;
'Modesto Ramirez' (West Central Front)—La Libertad, San Salvador, Cuscutlan, Chalatenango;
'Anastasio Aquino' (East Central Front)—La Paz, San Vicente, Cabañas;
'Francisco Sachez' (Eastern Front)—Usulatan, San Miguel, La Union, Morazán.

There were 6,500–7,000 full-time guerrillas in regular units; local guerrilla groups, whose part-time members combined fighting with their usual jobs; and support groups, providing information, supplies, evacuation and escape-routes.

In December 1980 US President Jimmy Carter suspended military aid to the Salvadorean Government in response to human rights abuses by the

Salvadorean infantry on the march, the soldier (right) carrying a mortar tube. (Vicente Talon)

Army, National Police and National Guard; and in January 1981 the guerrillas launched a country-wide general offensive. The Army, without the resources to retaliate, had to wait until July when Ronald Reagan's Republican administration, seeing in the guerrillas a Soviet-backed communist threat, resumed aid. The Army, by strictly applying the draft law, expanded its numbers and established new counter-insurgency units: the 'Immediate Reaction Infantry Battalions' (BIRIA), of which the 'Atlacatl' Battalion fought in the July counter-offensive, and in late 1983 the 'Cazadores' (Rangers).

The guerrillas achieved several diplomatic successes, notably the Franco-Mexican declaration of August 1981, recognising the FDR-FMLN as a legitimate force. In June 1982 FMLN guerrillas had seized control of Chalatenango Province (Central Salvador) and Morazán (Eastern Salvador), and established strong enclaves elsewhere, such as Volcan de Guazapa (San Salvador), which the Army scarcely dared enter. Guerrilla tactics included sabotaging lines of communication, public utilities, electrical and telephone lines; attacks on military bases and brigade HQs, often successful; and temporarily occupying towns, even pro-

Salvadorean troopers of the 'El Pilpil' Special Forces Battalion on the march, proudly displaying their maroon berets with battalion badge. (Vicente Talon)

vincial capitals. Despite Army counter-offensives the FMLN maintained the pressure through 1982 and into 1983. On 27 January 1982 it attacked the Air Force HQ at Ilopango Airbase, Central Salvador, destroying or damaging 12 aircraft and seven helicopters (almost 50 per cent of Air Force strength)—losses immediately made good by the United States. On 28 January 1983 they attacked I Brigade HQ near San Salvador. They now controlled one-third of the country, but were denied final victory by continuing US aid to the Salvadorean Army.

By mid-1983 the Army's position began to improve. Its numbers (15,000—1980 strength, 7,000) and US advisers, officially limited to 55, were transforming it into a force with three components: six brigades (formerly three) for static defence of towns and strategically important locations; heavily armed BIRIA Battalions, 1,100–1,400 strong, airportable, using Bell UH-1H helicopters in 'search and destroy' missions; and 14 Ranger Battalions, small (350–400 strong), lightly armed and mobile, distributed one per

province, trained in counter-insurgency at a local level. These troops were supported by programmes from the 'Civic-Military Action Institute' and 'National Commission for the Rebuilding of Areas'. Politically, the election of Christian Democrat José Napoléon Duarte in May 1983 avoided an intensification of hostilities between extreme-right paramilitary groups and the guerrillas. New 'low intensity war' tactics proposed by US advisers were intended to contain the guerrillas in certain provinces where they would be destroyed by the Army, and to promote civic action projects to discourage local support for the guerrillas.

Since 1984 US shipments of Hughes 500MD attack helicopters, Bell UH-1M helicopter gunships, Douglas C-47 'Puff the Magic Dragon' and A-37B ground-attack aircraft, modern technology, and improved training of Salvadorean troops, have enabled the Army to contain the guerrillas, swinging the balance in its favour since 1985, and thus bringing the war to a stalemate.

Once in power, Duarte began negotiations with

A Salvadorean armed escort for supplies bound for Santa Clara, centre of an operation against FMLN guerrillas in August 1982. (Vicente Talon)

the FDR-FMLN from the end of 1984; these ended without success, but were resumed in August 1987 after the 2nd Esquipulas Accord, with the same disappointing result. At present the FMLN cannot retain control of large areas, as in 1980, but can operate freely throughout the country, attacking the Army and the economic infrastructure, and is now strong enough to carry the wars to the towns.

FMLN guerrillas proudly display their red and white battle-flag to the villagers of San Francisco Javier, Usulután Province, captured from the Salvadorean Army the previous day, 25 January 1983. Two of the guerrillas wear complete military uniforms, only lack of insignia distinguishing them from government troops (Vicente Talon)

Mechanised infantry of the Salvadorean Cavalry Regiment wearing 'woodland' camouflage fatigues and carrying M16 rifles. (Julio Montes)

Current forces

The Army has 43,000 men, dividing the country into three Military Zones—West, Central and East, garrisoned by six Infantry Brigades (formerly regiments): 2nd Brigade (HQ Santa Ana) in the Western Zone; 4th (Chalatenango) and 5th (San Vicente) in Central; 3rd (San Miguel) and 6th (Usulutan) in Eastern. A Brigade has three or four infantry battalions (numbered internally 1st–4th), totalling 22 battalions. There are also seven independent 'Military Detachments', each two or three battalions strong—DM1 (Chalatenango), DM2 (Sensuntepeque), DM3 (La Union), DM4 (San Francisco Gotera), DM5 (Cojutepeque), DM6 (Sonsonate), DM7 (Ahuachapan) and the Engineer Detachment (Zacateroluca). Each brigade or detachment commander (a colonel) controls all Army and Police combat units in his area, including the 'Anti-Terrorist Reaction Infantry Battalions' (BIATs) formed in many garrisons and the 14 provincially allocated Ranger Battalions (e.g. 'Cazadores Jiboa', 'Cazadores Nonualco'). Independent units include the six 'BIRIAs'—'Atlacatl', 'Ramon Belloso', 'Atonal' (all formed 1980), 'Pipil', 'Manuel Jose Arce' (both formed 1983) and 'Eusebio Bracamonte'. Others are the 'Teniente Coronel Oscar Osorio' Artillery Regt. (three battalions), controlling the AA Defence Bn. (companies divided between Ilopango Airbase and 3rd Brigade); the Cavalry Regt. (two mechanised bns., HQ Coy., Recondo Group); the Airborne Bn. (Ilopango), since 1983 reverting to Army control; and two highly classified 'Special Forces Groups' (GOES)—1st 'Prial' (LRRP unit), 2nd 'Hacha' (SAS-type unit).

There is a 7,500-strong Air Force, and the 1,500-strong Navy includes the 600-strong '12 de Octobre' Marine Bn. (BIM) at Usulutan, and the 'Barracuda' and 'Piranha' Naval Commando companies (each 100 men) at La Union. There are also 7,600 National Guard (Rural Security), 6,000 National Police (Urban Security), 2,400 Treasury Police (Frontier Guards) and 17,000 Civil Defence (village militia). All are heavily involved in the war. Although training and morale has improved since 1980 the Armed Forces do not appear to be able to defeat 6,500–7,000 regular FMLN guerrillas.

El Salvador's future remains unclear. Duarte's terminal cancer forced him to withdraw from the March 1989 Presidential Elections, which were won by Roberto d'Aubuisson's extreme right-wing 'Nationalist Republican Alliance' party (ARENA). In September 1989 ARENA initiated negotiations with the FMLN, but with little success. The war has cost 70,000 lives (mostly reprisal victims rather than casualties of the fighting), and the exile of one quarter of the population. The government remains dependent on United States aid.

Honduras

This thinly populated, impoverished country is a haven of peace compared with the guerrilla wars devastating Guatemala, El Salvador and Nicaragua. The Honduran Armed Forces regularly intervene in politics, but not with the same brutality as in neighbouring countries; and the government, though basically conservative, is sensitive to developing social trends.

A guerrilla movement, the 'Cinchoneros', existed at the end of the last century, but the present level of guerrilla activity is minimal. Today's guerrilla organisations commenced operations in 1975, but were hardly noticed until the Sandinista victory in Nicaragua in July 1979. That year the 'People's Liberation Forces—Cinchoneros' (FPL-C) was formed; in 1980 the 'Morazán National Liberation Front' (FMLN), and in 1981 the 'Revolutionary People's Forces—Lorenzo Zelaya' (FPR-LZ). The Salvadorean PRTC is also active. In the early 1970s these groups carried out kidnappings and assassinations in the towns, and in 1987 agreed to co-ordinate activities.

The expansion of the Honduran Army (10,000 in 1980; 14,600 today) is not due to the guerrillas, but to a firm military alliance concluded with the Reagan administration. The United States has decided to transform Honduras into the 'aircraft-carrier' of the region. There are virtually continuous large US-Honduran military manoeuvres in counter-insurgency. The United States military presence is permanent in large bases such as Palmerola, and the Americans have financed a large road and airfield construction programme, with clear military implications. Although Honduras is traditionally hostile to El Salvador, the two armies collaborate in operations against Salvadorean FMLN guerrillas on Honduras's southern border, permitting the establishment of the 'Regional Military Training Centre' (CREM) in May 1983 to train Salvadorean battalions. Finally, Honduras hosts the main operational base of the Nicaraguan 'Contras', with thousands of men

Honduran Armed Forces Commander Gen. Gustavo Alvarez Martinez in 1986 with Honduran commanders in field uniform. Note the mixture of metal and subdued insignia, now uniformly subdued; and the 'duck-hunter' camouflage fatigues worn by the officer displaying jump-wings on his cap. See Plate E.

Alvarez at a press conference on 16 August 1983, announcing Honduras's invitation to United States troops to come to Honduras to help confront Sandinista incursions. (Vicente Talon)

along the eastern border, who regularly leave for offensive missions in Nicaragua.

Since 1980 there have been hundreds of border violations; the Sandinistas complain about 'Contra' incursions and unauthorised overflights in Nicaraguan airspace, the Hondurans about Sandinista units pursuing 'Contras' into Honduras— operations that were only opposed by the Honduran Army from the end of 1986.

In October 1986 the Honduran Army, US-trained and equipped, was easily able to mount a 2,500-man operation to prevent FPL-C starting a guerrilla war on the northern coast near La Ceiba, and between 7 and 11 December 1986 it repelled a Sandinista incursion into El Paraiso (South-East Honduras). These co-ordinated air-ground operations demonstrated improved Army effectiveness since its humiliation in the 1969 'Football War'.

The Honduran-Nicaraguan situation has been called 'undeclared war', and border incidents are increasing in seriousness, culminating in the March 1988 incident when US élite troops were rushed to Honduras to help repel what was thought to be a full-scale Sandinista invasion, and a large operation was mounted to expel the intruders. Never were Honduras and Nicaragua closer to war. In summer 1989, resulting from the agreements by the Central American Presidents,

Honduras decided to begin expelling the Contras from its territory.

Current forces

The 14,600-strong Honduran Army has three infantry brigades, each with one artillery and three infantry battalions; five independent infantry battalions; one armoured cavalry regiment (British Scorpion and Scimitar tanks, Saladin and Israeli RBY-1 armoured cars); one independent artillery regiment; one engineer battalion; the 'Special Force' (a battalion, formed 1973); and the Presidential Guard Company. The 'Cobra Police Squadron' (an airborne unit, since 1983 battalion-size) is under National Police control.

The presence of US troops and 'Contras', the alliance with the traditional enemy El Salvador, and the constant risk of a damaging war with Nicaragua, have all generated much tension in Honduras, evidenced by the hostile demonstration outside the United States Embassy in the capital, Tegucigalpa, in April 1988.

Nicaragua

The Nicaraguan Civil War, the longest and most intense in Central America, can be traced back to the rebellion against the long United States occupation, 1912–33. The liberal populist Gen. Augusto César Sandino led his 1,000-strong 'National Sovereignty Defence Army' (EDSN) from El Chipote, North-West Nicaragua, from 1926 until the United States withdrawal in 1933, when elections were held.

In 1925 the United States had established the *Guardia Nacional* with Anastasio 'Tacho' Somoza García as Chief Director. In 1934 Somoza had Sandino killed and on 2 June 1936 appointed himself president, deposing President Juan Sacusa; Somoza retained control of the Guard and crushed the EDSN, installing a corrupt dictatorship linked to US business interests. He died in 1956, and his elder son Luis Somoza Debayle succeeded as Chief Director and President; he died in 1962, and 'Tacho's' second son Anastasio 'Tachito' Somoza Debayle became Chief Director and in 1965 President.

This gangster regime soon earned the hatred of most sections of the population, leaving the Guard—which combined military and police functions—as its only powerbase. Efficient, brutal, constantly modernised, the Guard was the personal instrument of the Somoza family, 'an army occupying its own country'.

In 1962 Sandino's memory and Castro's success in Cuba led to the formation of the 'Sandinista National Liberation Front' (FSLN), whose initial rural and urban guerrilla successes were jeopardised by a Guard counter-offensive in 1963 in the Bocay region. The repression against the FSLN and other opposition groups increased in 1966. In 1967 hundreds of unarmed demonstrators were gunned down, causing an escalation in the war. In August 1967 National Guard operations in Pancasán (South-West Nicaragua) inflicted serious losses on the FSLN, forcing it to scale down its activities for several years; but anti-Somoza feeling continued unabated as Somoza's illegal methods were exposed, notably when the Guard pocketed

much of the international aid sent after the Managua earthquake of 23 December 1972.

The crisis of the 1970s

On 27 December 1974 the FSLN scored a huge propaganda coup by taking hostage, and ransoming, some top government officials and Turner B. Shelton, the United States Ambassador. The Guard responded with increased repression in the period 1975–6. In January 1978 Pedro Joaquin Chamorro, editor of the main opposition newspaper *La Prensa*, was murdered by the Guard; the resulting public indignation led to demonstrations and an unsuccessful general strike organised by the FSLN. In August there were popular uprisings in provincial towns, including Matagalpa, Jinotepa, Esteli and Masaya.

The FSLN, 500–1,000 strong in 1976, numbered in late 1978 3,000 regular guerrillas. It was divided into three 'tendencies'; the pluralist *Terceristas* (Third Force), including Christian, social democrat and middle-class opposition, formed in 1976 by Daniel and Umberto Ortega Saavedra and Eden Pastora Gómez, was the largest (2,000 guerrillas) and boldest, operating in southern Nicaragua. The Marxists—Tomás Borge's pro-

Entrenched Sandinista guerrillas defend Masaya City with captured M1 Garand rifles against determined but unsuccessful counterattacks by the Nicaraguan National Guard on 19 June 1979, in the final campaign of the war. (Vicente Talon)

A trooper of the élite Irregular Warfare Battalion *Coro de Angeles* ('Angels' Choir'—named after the young children who warned Sandino's army of approaching enemy units in the 1926–33 insurrection). He wears the distinctive Sandinista field hat derived from the Soviet tropical hat, and carries an AKM.

now entirely eliminate the FSLN.

Sandinistas date the beginning of the final campaign from 22 August 1978, when 25 *Tercerista* guerrillas, under Pastora ('Comandante Cero'—Commander Zero), occupied the National Palace, took 2,000 hostages, and escaped to Panama. The Carter administration in Washington tried to create a broad anti-Somoza political front from the FSLN and conservative UDEL and FAO political groups, but this plan foundered on 31 November 1978 when Somoza refused to stand down. Now there was no alternative to war.

On 4 May 1979 there were more armed uprisings in towns such as León, Matagalpa, Masaya and even Managua. The FSLN was now better organised militarily, and the Guard was forced to retreat to the Infantry Training School and Managua airport, Air Force HQ, where the FSLN besieged it. After 30 days the Guard regained control of Managua, but this could not alter the course of the war. Other towns were under siege, and more guerrilla columns moved from bases on the Costa Rican and Honduran borders and liberated areas in Central Nicaragua towards Managua, which 5,000 guerrillas and 15,000 supporting militia attacked. On 17 July Somoza and many Guard officers fled; the undefeated but demoralised Guard disintegrated, many enlisted men being taken prisoner when, on 19 July, the FSLN took Managua.

The Contra War

The fighting was not over, for a new guerrilla war, this time against the FSLN, began almost immediately. There were two reasons for this. When the Sandinista Junta tried to impose its radical Marxist beliefs on the broadly based Government of National Construction the non-FSLN parties opposed it, not wanting another dictatorship to succeed Somoza's. Then some non-Marxist leaders left the FSLN itself—in April 1980 Violeta Barrios de Chomorro, wife of the *La Prensa* editor murdered by the Guard, and Alfonso Robelo who, with Eden Pastora (who resigned in 1981), founded the ARDE 'Contra' group. Secondly, the Reagan administration saw the Sandinistas as a hardline communist regime supporting destabilising guerrilla movements in Central America, and stopped the 118 million dollar aid programme

Cuba 'Prolonged People's War' (GPP), former rural guerrillas, and Jaime Wheelock's Maoist 'Proletarians', formed in 1975 from former urban guerrillas—operated in the north.

In early 1978 the 7,000-strong Nicaraguan National Guard was organised for internal security with 16 infantry companies, the Presidential Guard Battalion, one mechanised company, one engineer battalion, a field artillery battery and an AA battery. The only tactical unit was the élite 700-strong 'Somoza Combat Battalion' under 'Tachito's' son, Maj. Anastasio Somoza Portocarrero. By July 1979 new recruits, trained at the 'Infantry Basic Training School' (EEBI), had swollen the Guard's strength to 14–15,000, some in new 'Special Counter-insurgency Brigades'. These forces, adequate to crush earlier revolts, could not voted by Congress in 1979.

Somoza's followers in exile, called 'Somocistas' by the Sandinistas, organised three groups of Contras (counter-revolutionaries) in 1980: the '15 September Legion', with senior Guard officers under Col. Enrique Bermudez Varela, former military attaché in Washington; the 'National Democratic Revolutionary Association' (ADREN), with junior officers; and the 'National Liberation Army' (ELN), with enlisted men. However, it was not until Ronald Reagan's presidency in January 1981 that they had the backing to commence operations. In fact the Contra war is a classic example of indirect external military intervention.

In 1982 these groups formed the 'Nicaraguan Democratic Force' (FDN) with Adolfo Calero Portocarrero as political leader and Bermudez as military commander. They established training bases in Guatemala and Florida and operational bases in Honduras. The FDN, 5,000 strong in 1982, 10–15,000 in mid-1984, operates in 'Detachments', 'Groups' and 200–250-strong 'Task Forces' (e.g. 'Task Force Pancasán'), grouped into 'Regional Commands' (e.g. 'Regional Command Quilali'; and the largest, 'Jorge Salazar 2', claiming 6,000 men in 1984). The 'Armed Forces of National Resistance' (FARN), under Fernando Chamorro, are allied to FDN.

In 1982 a second front was opened on the Costa Rican frontier with the formation of the 'Democratic Revolutionary Alliance' (ARDE) group under Robelo, and its military wing, the 3,000-strong 'Sandinista Revolutionary Front', led by Eden Pastora and organised in 'Zones' (under 'Comandantes'), columns, platoons and squads. The situation is further complicated by the establishment in 1981 of two guerrilla armies among the Miskito Indians of the east coast, a community which had suffered excesses at the hands of the Sandinistas—Steadman Fagoth Müller's 'Misura', allied to FDN/FARN, and Brooklyn Rivera's 'Misurasata', formed 1982 as a splinter group from 'Misura' and allied to 'ARDE' until 1984. In September 1985 a third Miskito group, 'Kisan', with 1,000–2,000 guerrillas, was formed by Diego

Sandinista Militia in characteristic light-tan uniforms pose for a photograph.

Wycliff after Fagoth successfully and Rivera unsuccessfully held peace-talks with the Sandinistas.

Although the Contras attempt to present a good public image, their genuinely libertarian elements are compromised by association with the pro-Somoza groups. Their level of activity increased from 15 attacks (1981), 78 (1982), to over 600 (1983). They concentrate on economic targets, the most notorious attack being the mining of Nicaraguan ports in 1983, which threatened to destroy the country's economy, and in which, according to the International Court in the Hague, the CIA were involved. There have been many violations of Nicaraguan airspace by aircraft supplying Contra field units, but including the bombing of Managua Airport in 1983.

As in Cuba, women serve in the Nicaraguan Sandinista Militia on an equal footing with men.

The Sandinistas have reacted to this threat by massively expanding their army—the *Ejercitó Popular Sandinista*, (EPS), formed 22 August 1980, and the *Milicia Popular Sandinista*, formed 20 February 1980—and by obtaining weapons from France (from December 1981) and the Soviet Union (often via Cuba) after United States aid ceased.

1983 was undoubtedly the Sandinistas' worst year, with constant Contra pressure from the Honduran and Costa Rican border areas, and United States intervention in Grenada (October 1983) widely interpreted as a rehearsal for an invasion of Nicaragua. By 1984 the FDN alone had 3,000 of its 15,000 men permanently stationed in Zelaya Department, Eastern Nicaragua. Attacks increased to 948, but this was a lower rate of increase than in 1983, and 1984 can now be seen as a turning point when the Sandinistas gained the initiative.

The government made a pact with some of the Miskito Indians, who now surrendered their weapons. On 30 May 1984 Eden Pastora escaped an assassination bomb, but was expelled from ARDE when, as a 'true Sandinista', he refused to ally with the 'Somocista' FDN, as required by the United States. Robelo took over ARDE command and made the alliance, but ARDE's strength declined. It was now obvious that, notwithstanding massive US aid, the Contra 'Freedom Fighters'—as United States officials called them—could not deliver the military success required in return for such a huge investment in training and equipment. Meanwhile the FSLN performed well in national elections, defeating the 'Democratic Convergence', a union of opposition parties.

The Sandinistas expected an increase in Contra pressure with the second Reagan administration starting January 1985, as the US president broke off the United States-Nicaraguan bilateral talks in Manzanillo (Mexico), imposing a trade embargo in April. In spite of the US Congress's suspension of Contra aid in 1984 the administration delivered 25 million dollars of aid, increasing to 100 million in 1986; but there was no corresponding Contra breakthrough, although attacks jumped to 1,367 (1985) and almost 3,000 (1986). ARDE guerrilla activity dwindled to virtually nothing, mainly due to a stricter interpretation of their neutrality by the

FDN Contra guerrillas, in 1984. Some wear the blue-green fatigues, others camouflage uniforms and webbing not dissimilar to those of the Sandinista enemy. They carry a mixture of US-supplied M16 and captured AKM weapons.

Costa Ricans. In the north EPS units were resisting Contra attacks and pursuing them to their Honduran bases, leaving a few small FDN groups in central and southern Nicaragua, entirely dependent on air-dropped supplies. From June 1985 tensions arose between ex-National Guardsmen and other Contras, all now officially federated in the 'National Opposition Union' (UNO). The United States was now switching support from the Contras to the Honduran Army, expecting an eventual war with Nicaragua. Border clashes between the two armies increased dramatically in 1986, reaching a level of 'undeclared war'.

By 1987 the efforts of the anti-Sandinista coalition were clearly in vain; the Contras could not achieve military victory, and though the economic blockade had severely damaged the Nicaraguan economy, it had not destroyed it. The Sandinistas abandoned their 'state of siege' and boldly proposed direct negotiations with the Contras. Contacts with the 'National Resistance' (RN), the new name for UNO, commenced at the end of 1987, but without appreciable success. In February 1988 the United States Congress finally prevented all Contra aid, forcing the RN to seek a negotiated settlement. The Sandinistas urgently needed peace, as the war (and government incompetence) had provoked a serious economic crisis and the

people, increasingly discontented, were turning to the opposition Democratic Convergence.

On 1 April 1988 the Sandinistas and RN concluded a ceasefire at Sapoa, valid for two months and renewable. This agreement was not welcomed by the US government nor by Bermudez, but was accepted by the rest of the RN and the Democratic Convergence. Talks about a permanent peace, held in Managua, were suspended in June through the intransigence of Bermudez's followers, and the Sandinistas now considered reopening hostilities to deal the final blow to the Contras before talks were resumed in Guatemala in September 1988. During 1989 'Contra' strength declined, as the new Bush Administration backed Honduran efforts to expel them from Honduran bases, and the Sandinista government began to liberalise.

Current forces

Nicaragua has seven Military Regions—1st (HQ Estelí) covering Estelí, Madriz and Nueva Segovia Departments; 2nd (Chinandega)—Léon, Chinandega; 3rd (Managua)—Managua; 4th (Mata-

Eden Pastora in 1984, both physically and politically a shadow of his former self, wearing a newly grown 'Castro' beard, but retaining his cap badge in Sandinista colours—red star on black disc, indicating his continued allegiance to the ideals of General Sandino.

'Jerman Pomares', 'Juan Pablo Umanzor', 'Santos López', 'Miguel Angel Ortez', 'Farabundo Martí' and 'Socrates Sandino' identified so far; and some Light Ranger Battalions (*Batallon Ligero Cazadores*, 'BLC'), e.g. 'BLC Gaspar García Laviana'. Some of the above units form the two mechanised brigades, each with one field artillery and three infantry battalions and two tank companies.

The 30,000 reservists are organised in 160 understrength battalions, including Reserve Infantry Battalions (using the Cuban four-digit numbering system, e.g. 25–21, 25–23, 47–10, 50–09, 50–11) organised in brigades (e.g. 31st Brigade) and Permanent Territorial Companies ('COPETEs'). There are 7,000 Border Guards (*Tropas Guardafronteras*, 'TGF') in seven battalions; a 2,000-strong brigade (*Tropas Pablo Ubeda*) equivalent to Soviet MVD troops, under the 'Directorate General of State Security' (DGSE); 1,000 Sandinista Navy personnel, 3,400 Sandinista Air Force, Sandinista Police, and 50,000 Militia in battalions and Territorial Brigades.

The United States objects to the size of the Armed Forces, at 130,000 almost nine times the former National Guard's maximum wartime strength; yet President Ortega talks of a 60,000–80,000 standing army and 600,000 reserves. It also points to Nicaragua's 175 tanks, suitable for an armoured thrust through the Choloteca Gap into Honduras, all suggesting an aggressive intent denied by Ortega.

The 24,000 Contras (active strength 12,000–15,000) have 12,000 FDN and 1,000 'Kisan' on the Northern Front (HQ Honduras), and 1,500–3,000 FARN, 500 'Misurasata' and 200 ARDE in the 'Southern Opposition Bloc' (HQ Costa Rica), but these numbers are reducing as dispirited Contras abandon a cause which seems to have no future.

galpa)—Matagalpa, Boaco Jinotega, western Zelaya; 5th (Puerto Cabezas)—northern Zelaya; 6th (Granada)—Carazo, Masaya, Rivas; 7th (Bluefields)—Chantales, Rio San Juan, southern Zelaya.

The EPS has 67,000 men, with 17,000 regulars (Active Military Service—SMA) and 20,000 two-year conscripts (Patriotic Military Service—SMP, instituted late 1983). There are four armoured battalions (Soviet T55 and PT-76 tanks), one mechanised battalion, one field artillery brigade (four bns.), four field artillery, one AA and four engineer battalions, and 'Special Duty Commandos (CODE). The 23 infantry battalions include one Airborne (formed 1982); at least nine 700-man anti-guerrilla Irregular Warfare Battalions (*Batallon de Lucha Irregular*, 'BLI')—'Simon Bolivar', 'Coro de Angeles', 'Ramón Raudales',

Costa Rica

This small country, the most stable democracy in Central America, has no serious political or social tensions and, since 1949, no conventional army. In 1948 the Costa Rican Army, numbering 339 in one infantry company and one artillery battery,

Cuba:
1: 1st Lt., 1st Regt. 'Cuatro de Septiembre', Inf. Div., 1958
2: Comandante Rebel Army, 1958
3: Coronel, Infantry, FAR, 1988

A

1: Cuba: Sgt., Infantry, FAR, 1988
2: Cuba: Warrant Officer, Marine Bn., 1988
3: Mexico: Sgt., Assault Bn., Presidential Guard, 1988

B

1: **Guatemala: Sgt., Special Forces Gp., 1988**
2: **Guatemala: Infantryman, 1st Military Zone, 1988**
3: **El Salvador: Col., Cavalry Regt., 1988**

El Salvador:
1: Sgt., National Guard, 1986
2: Capt., Infantry, 1988
3: Cpl., 'Jiboa' Ranger Bn., 1988
4: Sgt., Marine Inf. Bn., 1988

D

Honduras:
1: 1st Lt., 2nd Airborne Bn., 1986
2: 2nd Lt., 110th Inf. Bde., 1986
3: Police paratrooper, Cobra Bn., 1988

E

Nicaragua:
1: Cpl., Somoza Bn., National Guard, 1979
2: Comandante, FSLN, 1979
3: Capt., Sandinista People's Army, 1988
4: Sgt., 'Simon Bolivar' BLI, 1988

F

Nicaragua:
1: 'Contra' guerrilla, FDN, 1984
2: 'Contra', FDN 'Special Forces', 1988
3: 'Contra' guerrilla, ARDE, 1985

G

1: Costa Rica: 1st Lt., Northern Border Security Bn., 1988
2: Panama: 2nd Lt., 7th Fusilier Co., 1988
3: Haiti: Sgt., Presidential Guard, 1988
4: Haiti: National Security Volunteers militiaman, 1985

theoretically supported by 33 Militia battalions, backed President Teodoro Picado Michalski of the National Republican Party (PNR) in his refusal to leave office after an election defeat. José Figueres, leader of the Social Democrats, established a 'Caribbean Legion', which rose up in revolt to enforce the election result, and defeated the Army in a two-month civil war costing 1,600 lives. The 1949 Constitution abolished the Army, replacing it with the *Guardia Civil* as the only armed force.

In January 1955 the Central American dictators Somoza (Nicaragua) and Trujillo (Dominican Republic) supported an invasion of Costa Rica from Nicaragua by exiled supporters of former President Rafael Calderón Guardia, with Somoza supplying air-cover. This operation, seemingly a copy of the 1954 Guatemalan invasion which toppled President Arbenz, at first made good progress, occupying Ciudad Quesada in the north; but Figueres reacted quickly, mobilised 16,000 men and gained United States and Organisation of American States support. He retook Ciudad Quesada and drove the invaders back into Nicaragua. In 1978 and 1979 3,000 Costa Ricans were mobilised to repel incursions by Nicaraguan National Guards against Sandinista bases in Costa Rica.

Although Costa Rica had supported the Sandinistas, their July 1979 victory did not end tension with Nicaragua. The Costa Rican government, opposed to the radical excesses committed by the Sandinistas once they had gained power, permitted Eden Pastora's ARDE Contras to operate from Costa Rica in 1982–4. This change of policy towards the Sandinistas can also be attributed to United States pressure: since the 1970s economic crisis Costa Rica has been receiving massive US economic aid. Border tension has never reached Honduran levels, but the Sandinistas did complain about Costa Rica to the International Court in the Hague.

Even so, Costa Rica has worked hard to find a peaceful solution to the Nicaraguan conflict, notably at the June 1987 'Esquipulas Accords', which earned President Oscar Arias the Nobel Peace Prize.

Current forces

The Costa Rican Civil Guard, all volunteers, are commanded by a Director (a colonel) under the Ministry of Public Security. The force acts as an urban police force (rural policing is carried out by 3,500 Rural Guards) and a military force. The 6,000 men are organised in seven provincial companies (practically small battalions)—San José, Alajuela, Cartago, Heredia, Guanacaste, Puntarenas and Limón; a battalion-sized Presidential Guard; and two light battalions—the 750-man Northern Border Security Battalion, trained by US Special Forces, to guard the border with Nicaragua; and a counter-insurgency battalion to confront the estimated 900 anti-government guerrillas (three groups). The 3,000-strong National Reserve was mobilised in 1955, 1978 and 1979. There is a General Staff, equipment for 10,000 reservists, a small coastguard (four patrol-boats) and an Air Unit (11 light aircraft, three helicopters).

Panama

The United States was directly involved in the revolt leading to Panama's independence from Colombia on 6 November 1903; and in return was allowed, under the 18 November 1903 Treaty, to build the Panama Canal (opened August 1914) and bisect the country with the 'Canal Zone', under US garrison. The United States has repeatedly intervened in Panamanian politics, and US forces have been sent in on 26 occasions. United States Army Southern Command is based in the Canal Zone, responsible for all the American continent south of the US-Mexican border, while the 'School of the Americas' (established 1946, under Panamanian control since 1 October 1984) has trained generations of Latin-American soldiers in anti-guerrilla tactics.

Panama's persistent demands to regain sovereignty of the Canal and Canal Zone have caused stormy relations with the United States, especially during 1964; but the country is inextricably tied economically to the United States, and has usually followed a pro-US policy.

On 11 October 1968 Col. Omar Torrijos Herrera, commander of the *Guardia Nacional*—formed in 1953 from the National Police, which had itself

were more critical of the United States than were the civilian politicians, especially those in opposition. Although US trained and equipped, it resisted United States pressure to declare an anti-FMLN line in El Salvador or an anti-Sandinista line in Nicaragua. In 1983 Gen. Noriega became commander of the Guard, which was in 1984 renamed *Fuerzas de Defensa*, and publicly denounced President Reagan's Central American policy. In 1987 the United States pressured for the dismissal of Noriega, who was wanted in the USA on drug-trafficking charges. Relations reached a crisis in spring 1988, but threats of economic blockade or military intervention were presented by Noriega as a tactic to renege on the 1977 Treaty and prevent transfer of the Canal. The FD closed ranks behind him and Noriega is still firmly in power.

As in Costa Rica, the Defence Forces fulfil military and police functions, especially riot-control and internal security. The 1977 Treaty charges the force with the defence of the Canal after 1999, and so it has shifted emphasis from

Panamanian Gen. Torrijos in 1980, wearing olive green fatigues, gold branch (the rank badge, now four stars) on green 'combat-leader' shoulder loops.

replaced the Army in 1904—seized power in a coup, and formally requested transfer of Canal and Zone. Although the Guard had defeated a landing by 80 Cuban guerrillas in April 1959, and in the early 1960s had crushed an incipient rural guerrilla movement, it was not politically re-actionary. Torrijos had indoctrinated it with his own ideology—'Torrijism', a mixture of nationalism and populism. After years of tough negotiations the Torrijos-Carter Treaty of 7 September 1977 provided for the transfer of the Canal Zone on 1 October 1979 and total US withdrawal on 31 December 1999.

On 31 July 1981 the charismatic Gen. Torrijos was killed in a mysterious aeroplane crash. He was succeeded as Guard Commander by Florencio Florez, but Panama entered a period of political turmoil. Nominally under civilian control, the Guard held the real power, and its Torrijist officers

Policemen of the Panamanian National Guard in standard uniform (green hats and trousers, light grey shirts, gold insignia), only their whistles, pistols and night-sticks indicating their police duties.

internal security to national defence, still with US training and equipment—although internal unrest, especially since Noriega took command, has forced expansion of anti-riot units.

Current forces

The Defence Forces are voluntary, with 5,200 men on military duties. 4,500 men serve in seven 'Fusilier Companies (infantry)—1st 'Tigre' airmobile (HQ Panamá Vieja); 2nd 'Pumas' airportable (Tocumén Airport, Panama City); 3rd 'Diablo Rojo' (Chiriqui Province); 4th 'Urraca' (Central Barracks, Panama City); 5th 'Victoriano Lorenzo' (Fort Amador, Canal Zone); 6th 'Expedicionaria' (Rio Hato); 7th 'Macho de Monte' Ranger (Tocumén Airport). There are also a Presidential Guard, ceremonial cavalry squadron, Special Force company and two 700-man infantry battalions, one jungle-trained. There is a 500-man Navy; a 200-man Air Force (two squadrons); and 3,000 personnel on police duties, dispersed across the ten Military Zones, or in special units such as the Public Order Company for riot control.

Haiti

A black, French-speaking nation, the poorest in the Western Hemisphere, Haiti won independence from Napoleonic France on 1 January 1804 under Jean-Jacques Dessalines[1]. From July 1915 to 21 August 1934 it was occupied by the US Marine Corps, which replaced the Haitian Army on 24 August 1916 with the 2,650-man *Gendarmerie d'Haiti* for counter-insurgency duties, under Maj. Smedley Butler, USMC. After several redesignations it became *Armée Haitien* in 1963. From 22 October 1957 until his death on 21 April 1971 François 'Papa Doc' Duvalier was president, from 1964 'President for Life', a title assumed by his son and successor, Jean-Claude 'Baby Doc' Duvalier, until his overthrow on 7 February 1986.

[1] See Men-at-Arms 211, *Napoleon's Overseas Army*.

The Presidential Guard crew of the anti-aircraft gun the paranoid 'Papa Doc' Duvalier had sited in the grounds of the Presidential Palace, 1970.

Haitian troops in 1980 wearing uniforms still current. Note the triangular Presidential Guard shoulder patch, and collar cypher.

The 7,600-strong voluntary Haitian Army fulfils military and police functions, but its conventional military value is very low. There are nine Military Departments of which three are based in the capital, Port-au-Prince—the 500-man Presidential Guard (one infantry bn., one armoured sqn.), the Dessalines infantry battalion (seven companies) and the blue-uniformed Port-au-Prince Police (six companies). The North, North-West, Centre, West, South and Artibonite Departments each have a garrison detachment, totalling 21 companies, operating as district police. There are also a two-battery artillery battalion, Port-au-Prince Fire Brigade, Prison Guard Company, Coastguard (325 men) and Air Force (275). Only the Presidential Guard, Dessalines Battalion, and élite 'Leopards' Battalion (three companies, formed in 1971 for anti-guerrilla warfare, directly under the Chief-of-Staff) have any military value.

In the late 1950s 'Papa Doc' Duvalier formed the 15,000-strong National Security Volunteers, from 1971 under nominal army control, as a counterweight to the Army; and also the notorious 'Tontons Macoutes' secret police, to eliminate political opponents.

On 19 June 1988 Lt. Gen. Henri Namphy, Chief-of-Staff, overthrew the civilian President, Leslie Manigat, who had tried to dismiss him, ending a brief experiment in democracy, only to be ousted himself on 18 September 1988 by Brig. Gen. Prosper Avril, backed by Army NCOs and the 'Dessalines' Battalion. Although Haiti is poor and oppressed, there is currently no guerrilla movement.

Dominican Republic

Like Haiti, the Dominican Republic was from 29 November 1916 to September 1924 occupied by the US Marine Corps, which in 1917 replaced the Army with the Dominican Constabulary Guard, in 1928 renamed Dominican National Army, under Chief-of-Staff Lt. Col. Rafael Léonidas Trujillo Molina. On 23 February 1930 Trujillo was elected President, establishing a ruthless, corrupt dictatorship until his assassination on 30 May 1961.

Claiming a possible Haitian invasion (Haiti had occupied the country 1794–1809 and 1821–44 but, although hostile, was too weak to invade) and the precedent of Castro's Cuban revolution, Trujillo built up the most powerful armed forces in the region (16,500 men), really intended to suppress internal opposition. He easily defeated an attack by Cuban-backed exiles in July 1959; and boasted of being able to bomb Havana to ashes with his Boeing B-17 bombers, and of a swift occupation of Haiti.

After Trujillo's death the country lapsed into political turmoil. On 25 September 1963 a military coup deposed the left-wing President Professor Juan Bosch; but in April 1965 Bosch's Army supporters, the 'Constitutionalists', rebelled under Col. Francisco Caamaño Deñó. Fearing another Castro-style regime, President Lyndon B. Johnson sent in 23,000 US troops on 28 April 1965, offering to prevent a civil war between Caamaño's supporters and the bulk of the Army, under Gen. Eliás Wessín y Wessín and Gen. Antonio Imbert Barrera. The fighting continued; and on 6 May the Organisation of American States sent 2,000 Brazilian, Paraguayan, Honduran, Nicaraguan National Guard and Costa Rican troops to join the US Army (now 18,000 strong) as the 'Interamerican Pacification Force' (FIP). Fighting between rival factions and against the FIP lasted until August 1965. The FIP withdrew in September 1966, when Joaquín Balaguer was re-elected president and Caamaño and Wessín exiled. Some 3,000 Dominicans died in this civil war.

Since the war successive civilian governments have kept the Dominican Armed Forces out of politics. In February 1973 Col. Caamaño landed on the island to begin a guerrilla movement, but was killed in battle after a few days.

The Dominican Army, numbering 13,000 volunteers, is much less important than in Trujillo's time. There are four brigades (17 bns.), one artillery, one armoured, one Presidential Guard, and one engineer battalion. The obsolete equipment is being modernised. The 4,600-strong Navy includes a Marine battalion and a Naval Commando unit; the 3,765-strong Air Force has light aircraft, transports, helicopters, a parachute battalion and an AA battalion; and there are 10,000 National Police under an Army officer as Director-General.

The Plates

A1: Cuba: Teniente Primero, 1st 'Cuatro de Septiembre' Regt., Infantry Division, 1958
Cuban officers wore US-style uniforms copied by local tailors in better quality cloth, often with 18 carat gold insignia privately purchased from the San Ambrosio PX—the Cuban Harrods. Field service uniform was the US olive drab herringbone-twill fatigues with khaki-painted M1 helmet. This officer's khaki barrack dress has US pattern branch insignia on the hat and collar points (with regimental number) and branch-colour hat-cords: infantry, crossed rifles (green

cords); cavalry, crossed sabres (yellow); artillery, crossed cannons (red); engineers, castle (crimson). Cloth embroidered unit patches were sometimes worn on upper arms and metal rank insignia on shoulder straps: three five-pointed stars vertically placed for *General*; two—*Mayor General*; one—*General de Brigada*; three brass stars in a triangle—*Coronel*; two horizontally—*Teniente Coronel*; one—*Comandante*; three brass chevrons point down—*Capitán*; two—*Teniente Primero*; one—*Segundo Teniente*; one (gap at point)—*Subteniente* (equivalent US Chief Warrant Officer); one horizontal bar—*Suboficial* (Warrant Officer). Enlisted ranks wore US M1903 '10-pouch' webbing, trousers and canvas gaiters, carrying the M1903 Springfield rifle, or the Garand. They omitted collar badges and wore US-style buff chevrons point-up on olive green backing on upper arms: three chevrons, two 'rockers'—*Sargento de Primera*; with one rocker—*Sargento de Segunda*; three chevrons only—*Sargento de Tercera*; two chevrons, one rocker—*Cabo de Primera*; two chevrons—*Cabo*; one chevron—*Soldado de Primera*; no insignia—*Soldado Raso*. Officers' service dress was the US-style khaki peaked cap and tunic with the same insignia; the cap badge was the national crest on a trophy of arms in a wreath of brass or gold-embroidered, and a plain brass shield for enlisted men.

A2: Cuba: Comandante, Rebel Army; Escombray Mountains, early 1958
Conforming to traditional worldwide guerrilla practice, rank and file usually wore civilian clothes—coloured shirt, trousers, stout boots, straw hat or 'revolutionary' dark beret, with captured or improvised weapons and equipment. Guerrilla leaders encouraged a more uniformly military appearance, with US Army surplus clothing—olive green fatigue shirts and trousers, the M1943 'Walker cap', as favoured by Castro, with or without the stiffened crown, or captured M1 helmets. Brass Cuban Army rank insignia was worn on the cap only: a star—*Comandante* (company commander); three chevrons point down—*Capitán* (platoon leader); two chevrons—*Teniente* (squad leader). As victory approached, coloured arm-badges or armbands were worn, usually in Cuban red, white and blue; this example commemorates Castro's '20 July Movement'. This

Comandante has allowed his hair and beard to grow, 'to be shaved off when Cuba is free'; he wears captured M1903 webbing and sports a .45 cal. M3 'grease-gun'.

A3: Cuba: Coronel, Revolutionary Army, Infantry; barrack dress, 1988

In 1959 Castro introduced a green officers' service dress, retaining Batista's cap badge, and continuing the olive green fatigues and 'Walker cap' for combat dress. Officers' rank insignia were worn on jacket shoulder straps and field shirt collars: one star—*Comandante* (the highest rank, later expanded to five ranks); and four-one chevrons point down or one bar, all in brass, for junior officers. NCOs retained Batista's US chevrons. On 1 December 1973 conventional field and general ranks were introduced, and by 1980 the present markedly Soviet-style uniform. Officers and regular NCOs wear a drab brown service dress tunic with gold shield-in-wreath lapel-badges (generals, a gold star in a wreath with a laurel branch collar badge); a brown, black-peaked cap, with gold chin-cords (black strap for NCOs), green band, and national cap badge above a gold star with the gold initials 'FAR' on red boss. On barrack dress red Soviet collar patches edged gold are adorned with gold miniature cap-badge devices. The stiff Soviet-type shoulder-boards have olive green Russia braid for generals, with gold leaves below a white star on a red (left)/blue (right) rhomboid for *Comandante en Jefe* (Castro), or gold five-pointed stars: four—*General de Ejércitó*, three—*General de Cuerpo*; two—*General de División*; one—*General de Brigada*. Field officers have olive green braid, two vertical red centre stripes, and small gold stars: three—*Coronel*; two—*Teniente Coronel*; one—*Mayor*; company officers one stripe and four stars—*Capitán*; three—*Primer Teniente*; two—*Teniente*; one—*Subteniente*. Warrant Officers (senior regular NCOs) have red piping and small gold stars vertically placed: three—*Suboficial Primero*; two—*Suboficial*, and *Sargento de Primera* (Staff Sgt.) has four horizontal gold bars on a uniform-colour shoulder board. Conscripts wear an olive green blouse with field shoulder boards, branch shield on the upper sleeves and olive green 'Walker cap' with gold chin strap and national shield-in-wreath cap badge.

B1: Cuba: Sargento de Segunda; combat dress, 1988

All ranks wear a Soviet-style fatigue tunic or shirt, trousers and service dress rank insignia: for conscripts a stiff shoulder strap slide with yellow 'FAR' below three yellow bars—*Sargento de Segunda*; two bars—*Sargento de Tercera*; one—*Cabo*; none—*Soldado*. Headdress is a plain 'Walker cap', and a Cuban-manufactured Soviet M40 or Bulgarian M72 helmet. A Soviet 7.62 mm AKM assault rifle is carried with Soviet webbing—ammunition pouch on right hip, first-aid pouch and gasmask on left. Officers wear a brown leather 'Sam Browne' belt. Tank crews wear Soviet helmets and black coveralls, paratroopers a camouflage overall with cloth helmet. A Czech-style peaked flapped camouflage field cap is being introduced with a camouflaged field tunic and trousers for infantry, with rank insignia on shoulder-slides as here.

B2: Cuba: Primer Suboficial, Marine Battalion; barrack dress, 1988

The 550-strong élite *Desambarco del Granma* ('Granma Landing Unit'—commemorating the ship in which Castro reached Cuba in December 1956) wears Soviet-style black Marine uniforms. This long-service NCO wears officer's type cap badge (enlisted men omit the wreath) and 'Sam Browne' belt. Naval rank insignia is identical to the Army's, but field, company and warrant officers wear yellow braid shoulder boards with gold stars and black stripes, enlisted men black boards with yellow bars and 'FAR' title.

B3: Mexico: Sargento Segundo, Assault Troops Battalion, Presidential Guards Brigade; sentry uniform, 1988

Officers wear dark blue service dress (called 'Azul Z') with three-button plain cuff patches. The cap has the national cockade (green-white-red outer) above the hat band rank insignia. Brass jacket collar branch insignia (branch-colour for enlisted rank insignia) are: crossed rifles, trumpet (scarlet)—infantry; crossed sabres, helmet (bright blue)—cavalry; crossed sabres, tank (grey)—armour; crossed cannons, grenade (crimson)—artillery; castle (cobalt blue)—engineers; national crest (eagle, serpent, wreath) on eight-pointed star—Presidential Guards, with appropriate unit numbers or badge behind for different sub-units. Shoulder board rank insignia: four vertical silver five-pointed stars above gold national crest—*General de División* (Minister of Defence); three stars—*General de División*; two stars—*General de Brigada*; one star—*General Brigadier*. Three brass stars only, in a triangle—*Coronel*; two horizontally—*Teniente Coronel*; one—*Mayor*; three vertical linked brass bars—*Capitán Primero*; three (middle bar half-size)—*Capitán Segundo*; two—*Teniente*; one—*Subteniente*. Enlisted ranks wear OG107 fatigues (shown here) with black horizontal shoulder-strap bars (Presidential Guards—gold diagonal cuff stripes) on branch-colour backing: three—*Sargento Primero*; two—*Sargento Segundo*;

one—*Cabo*; one vertical bar (Pres. Gd., stripe on left sleeve only)—*Soldado de Primera*; no insignia—*Soldado*.

This Special Forces NCO guarding the National Palace wears an M1 helmet-liner with the national crest on the front, and unit patches on both sides—repeated on both upper sleeves; gold Guards collar patch with battalion badge (a figure of a combat soldier) on infantry scarlet; white

Central American armies have few ceremonial uniforms even for generals; these Guatemalan officers are exceptional. President Kjell Laugurud Garcia (right, smiling) is pictured in 1974 with senior officers, wearing the flamboyant black and gold dress uniform.

Salvadorean General José Guillén García, Minister of Defence and Security, in green service dress and Ministry of Defence shoulder patch (yellow star in green wreath on red-edged blue disc), talks to young officers in olive green field uniform with subdued insignia, 1984. (Vicente Talon)

ceremonial scarf, gloves and bootlaces. He wears US partial 'ALICE' webbing, and carries a West German G3 rifle. In combat a camouflage uniform and helmet cover are worn.

C1: Guatemala: Sargento Tecnico, Special Forces Group; combat dress, 1988
As in most of Central America, Guatemalan uniforms are heavily US influenced. Officers wear a black ceremonial peaked cap and tunic with gold embroidered insignia, or a green or light tan service tunic with matching peaked cap; the gold cap badge is a dove holding an independence-scroll over crossed rifles in a wreath. Generals have heavy red shoulder boards edged gold, with vertical gold stars above a gold cap badge: two—*General de División*; one—*General de Brigada*. Field officers wear vertically placed linked brass stars on plain straps: three—*Coronel*; two—*Teniente Coronel*; one—*Mayor*; company officers wear horizontally placed linked brass bars: three with brass star

superimposed—*Capitán Primero*; three—*Capitán Segundo*; two—*Teniente*; one—*Subteniente*. Brass collar branch badges are: crossed rifles—infantry; crossed sabres—armour; crossed cannons and grenade—artillery; castle—engineers; gold laurel leaf on a gold-edged red rhomboid—generals. Unit shields appear on left upper sleeves.

Enlisted ranks wear light tan shirt and trousers, and unit shields above US-style yellow chevrons point up on both upper arms: five chevrons and rocker—*Sargento Mayor*; four and rocker—*Sargento Tecnico*; three and rocker—*Sargento Primero*; three—*Sargento Segundo*; two—*Cabo*; one—*Soldado de Primera*; no insignia—*Soldado de Segunda*.

In combat olive green, US BDU 'woodland', or (as here) South Korean 'wavy' camouflage fatigues are worn with matching beret, 'boonie hat', bush hat, or Israeli OR201 Kevlar helmet (camouflaged brown and sand for paratroopers). A national flag patch is worn on the upper right sleeve, and officers wear subdued black collar rank insignia (laurel leaf for generals). Special Forces wear a red beret with 'KAIBIL' title above unit badge or (as here) rank badge; Marines a black beret, paratroopers a black beret with silver jump-wings above a company badge; otherwise, insignia are discouraged in the field. This SF trooper, his neat appearance suggesting urban security duty or a short-range operation, wears US M1956 webbing, and carries the Israeli UZI; the Galil and the M16 are also used.

C2: Guatemala: Infantryman, 1st Military Zone; combat dress, 1988

This squad machine gunner, armed with the US M60, wears partial M1967 webbing. Both US BDUs and less substantial copies appear to be worn by Guatemalan troops. This man's only insignia is the arm patch of the 1st Military Zone ('General Luis Garcia Leon') to which his battalion is subordinated. The pack appears to be the US nylon tropical rucksack.

C3: El Salvador: Coronel, Cavalry Regiment; service dress, 1988

Salvadorean officers wear copies of the US Army M1957 green dress uniform or the M1942 khaki equivalent, but with the distinctive national cuff of pointed, buttoned design. Rank insignia are worn on the shoulder straps: gold embroidered upright laurel leaf—*General*; three vertically placed brass stars—*Coronel*; two—*Teniente Coronel*; one—*Mayor*; three linked horizontal brass bars—*Capitán*; two—*Teniente*; one—*Subteniente*; one black—*Cadete*. Brass branch collar insignia follow US pattern: crossed rifles—infantry; crossed sabres—armoured cavalry; crossed cannons—artillery; castle—

engineers; crossed flags—signals. The unit badge is worn in coloured enamels on a right pocket fob, and its design is repeated in the left shoulder sleeve patch. The parachute wings above the left breast pocket follow the US shape with an added national cap badge motif.

D1: El Salvador: Sub-Sargento, National Guard; field service dress, 1986

Formed in 1912 as a rural police force, the *Guardia Nacional* is organised into 14 Provincial Companies (in practice, often battalion-sized) organised in five 'Commands': an MP Company; the '15 de Septiembre' BIAT; a Technical Assistance Dept. (US advisers and 'SWAT'); a Transport Group; and 'COPARA', a rapid-reaction anti-terrorist company. Until Army involvement in 1980 this often brutally efficient force bore the brunt of the guerrilla war.

This obsolete-looking uniform, inspired by the Spanish *Guardia Civil* on which the force was modelled, is still worn; but US jungle utilities or BDUs are often seen in the field. The gloss-black M1 helmet liner bears the national-coloured shield on the right side, and on the front the Army cap badge flanked by 'G' and 'N', in gold. 'GN' cypher badges are worn on both collars, and blue and

A parade of soldiers from the Salvadorean Army's 1st Infantry Brigade, with three kinds of fatigue uniform on view – OG107 jungle fatigues and two styles of 'woodland' camouflage. Note the green scarves worn as an unofficial sub-unit distinction. (Julio Montes)

Two 'COPARA' police troopers pose in field uniform, the left-hand man in US-style BDU camouflage and the right-hand man in olive jungle utilities; weapons are the M79 grenade-launcher and M60 machine gun. In the right background can be seen a trooper in the old-fashioned uniform illustrated as Plate D1. (Julio A. Montes)

white National Guard patches on both shoulders; sleeve rank insignia follow Army sequence. The US M1964-shape 'baseball' cap is also worn, with miniature metal rank insignia above the same badge as worn on the collar. The weapon here is the G3 rifle, with which this NCO has won the marksmanship badge on the left breast.

D2: El Salvador: Capitán, Infantry, San Salvador Province; field parade dress, 1988

Field uniform for all ranks consists of US-supplied OG107 cotton sateen shirt and trousers, or M1967 jungle utilities. The M1 helmet is often worn with loose string netting; the bush hat, 'boonie hat', and M1964 'baseball' cap are all worn, the latter with subdued officers' or brass NCOs' insignia, or unofficial unit badges. Officers wear black sub-dued rank insignia on the right collar, black branch badges on the left. The parade neck scarf is light blue for infantry, Rangers and Special Forces; apple green for General Staff; black for armour; olive green for paratroops; red for artil-lery; yellow for engineers; and orange for signals. Unit patches, when worn, are applied to both upper arms.

D3: El Salvador: Cabo, 'Jiboa' Cazador Battalion, San Vicente Province; combat dress, 1988

Élite units—Rangers (Cazadores), paratroops, Marine infantry, and Special Forces—wear a camouflage 'boonie hat' or M1967 beret; US-supplied (or locally bought copies of) 'woodland', or South Korean 'wavy' camouflage fatigues are normal. Standard Army webbing is M1956, but élite units have received some ALICE pattern equipment. On normal Army olive utilities US-style chevrons are worn on both upper sleeves: three chevrons and a rocker—Sargento; three chevrons—Sub-Sargento; two—Cabo; none—Soldado. In the field, élite units discourage the use of insignia, like the gold-on-black 'CAZADOR' title and brass rank insignia seen on this Ranger's black beret; metal battalion insignia are also sometimes worn below the Ranger qualification title by privates. Note US jungle boots and M79 grenade-launcher.

D4: El Salvador: Sub-Sargento, Marine Infantry Battalion; barrack dress, 1988

The Batallón de Infanteria de Marina, formed in 1985, is based at Usulatán on the swampy coastal border with Honduras, operating from US LCM-6 and -8 landing craft to prevent Nicaraguan weapons shipments reaching the FMLN guerrillas. Under Naval command, the BIM use Army ranks and élite unit uniforms. The black beret bears here the unit patch and rank insignia; the shoulder of the US BDUs bears a subdued version of the insignia, sometimes worn in combat. In the field the 'boonie hat' or a black 'SEAL-style' headscarf are worn, with standard US webbing and weapons.

E1: Honduras: Teniente, 2nd Airborne Battalion; combat dress, 1986

Combat dress for most Honduran troops consists of US-supplied OG107 cotton sateen shirt and trousers, or M1967 jungle utilities, with the M1 helmet or M1964 'baseball cap'; officers usually wear subdued black-on-olive rank and branch insignia on right and left collars, and enlisted ranks yellow sleeve chevrons. This élite paratrooper, sent to the border in December 1986 to oppose San-dinista 'hot pursuit' of Nicaraguan Contra units, wears an apparently personally acquired re-tailored version of US BDUs, cut as a light shirt with slanted pockets in jungle utility style, and a beret of the same material. Insignia include his rank bars on a branch-colour diamond patch below US jump-wings; a subdued Army shoulder patch in olive and black; and slanted name and national tabs on the chest. He wears ALICE webbing, the pouches pushed back on the hips; note pistol holster, knife and grenades. The weapon is the M16, with a black sling rigged assault-style. Note also the Israeli OR201 para-helmet, with a cover of 'duck hunter' camouflage.

E2: Honduras: Subteniente, 110th Infantry Brigade; combat dress, 1986

Photographed during the same operation as E1, this officer wears a complete uniform of shirt, trousers and beret in 'duck-hunter' camouflage, presumably acquired personally or at unit level. Insignia are the subdued rank and branch badges in black on olive, on the collars; a full-colour Army patch on the right sleeve; US 'Ranger' qualification title, in subdued form, and Honduran equivalent 'Teson' title, in full colours, on the left

shoulder; and what is presumably a diamond-shaped unit patch in black on OD, half obscured on the left pocket. He has a name tape on the right breast, but no national title opposite. His equipment is of US ALICE pattern, with the early belt buckle. We reconstruct the legs and jungle boots.

Honduran officers' service dress is based on US Army M1957 greens; a khaki equivalent is worn in summer. The peaked cap has a gold chin strap and brass national badge. Brass 'RH' cyphers and US-style branch insignia are worn on the collars and lapels: crossed rifles for infantry, special forces and paratroops; crossed sabres, crossed cannons, and a castle for armoured cavalry, artillery and engineers. On the shoulder straps officers wear brass vertically placed stars: five—*General de División*; four—*General de Brigada*; three—*Coronel*; two—*Teniente-Coronel*; one—*Mayor*. Company officers wear linked horizontal brass bars: three, two and one for *Capitán*, *Teniente*, and *Subteniente*.

Four FPL-FM guerrillas, three wearing neckerchiefs to hide their identities, during a press facility for visiting journalists, 1981. (Vicente Talon)

Nicaraguan President Somoza (right) confers with advisers after the Managua earthquake of December 1972. Note the US-supplied campaign hats and khaki uniforms, common amongst Central American armies from c. 1920 to 1970, and the M1943 stiffened 'Walker cap'.

Enlisted ranks wear US-style yellow chevrons on green backing on the upper sleeves of khaki uniform shirts, and on combat fatigues: three chevrons, solid diamond, three rockers—*Sargento Mayor*; three chevrons, three rockers—*Sargento Primero*; three chevrons, two rockers—*Sargento Segundo*; three chevrons, one rocker—*Sargento*; two chevrons—*Cabo*; one chevron—*Soldado de Primera*; none—*Soldado*.

E3: Honduras: Police paratrooper, Cobra Battalion, 1988
Formed as the *Cobra Policial Escuadron* in April 1979, this para-trained unit of the Public Security Forces was expanded to battalion strength in 1983. It is a rapid-intervention gendarmerie unit, and this uniform was photographed during anti-riot duty in Tegucigalpa in April 1988. The US BDUs have been modified in this unit by the addition of black shoulder straps and reinforcement at knees and elbows; and the pockets (including the flaps of

the rear trouser pockets) are also dyed black. Army-style chevrons are worn on the fatigues where appropriate; the cap is the Army's woodland-camouflage cap dyed black. The left shoulder patch has a gold and blue hooded cobra motif. The equipment is ALICE pattern, here with extra musettes for a range of grenades, and the gasmask; standard weapons are the CAR15 and the Browning GP35 automatic.

F1: Nicaragua: Cabo, Somoza Combat Battalion, Nicaraguan National Guard; combat dress, January 1979
The *Guardia Nacional* officers' service dress was the US-supplied M1942 khaki peaked cap with brown-japanned chin strap and peak, or black dress cap with gold chin strap, black peak with gold embroidery for field and general ranks, and silver triangular national cap badge. The khaki tunic had the cap badge on the collar and brass US-style lapel insignia: crossed rifles—infantry; crossed sabres—armour; crossed cannons—artillery; castle—engineers. Generals' shoulder strap rank insignia was five vertically placed five-pointed silver stars for *General de División*; four—*Mayor General*; three—*General de Brigada*; field officers wore brass stars: three—*Coronel*; two—*Teniente Coronel*; one—*Major*; company officers wore horizontal linked brass bars: three—*Capitán*; two—*Teniente*; one—*Subteniente*. Enlisted ranks wore yellow on dark-green chevrons.

Combat uniform was the OG107 cotton sateen shirt and trousers or, as here, M1967 jungle utilities, with subdued black officers' rank insignia on the right collar, branch insignia on the left, and yellow chevrons for NCOs. A subdued name-tape was worn over the right breast pocket, the national title over the left, and unit patches on both upper sleeves. For field parade a branch-colour neck scarf was added (light blue for infantry). This NCO wears M1956 webbing; note also magazine bandoliers, Israeli 5.56 mm Galil assault rifle, smoke grenades, and Israeli OR201 Kevlar helmet.

F2: Nicaragua: Comandante, Sandinista National Liberation Front; Managua, June 1979
FSLN clothing and weapons procurement followed the familiar pattern of its model, Castro's Rebel Army (see plate A2). Rank and file (*Combatientes*) wore civilian clothes, often with 'Cuban'-

style beards and long hair. Leaders (*Comandantes*) like the charismatic Eden Pastora pictured here, favoured a more conventionally military appearance. Cuba supplied olive green fatigue shirts, trousers, and the characteristic peaked field cap copied from the US M1943 'Walker cap'. Pastora, leading the non-Marxist *Terceristas*, is wearing some of these uniform items with captured US M1956 webbing, and the US M1911 Colt .45 in a shoulder rig. He also appears to have a slung AK rifle, and a haversack—possibly a Soviet gasmask satchel? No national, rank or unit insignia were worn.

F3: Nicaragua: Capitán, Sandinista People's Army; field parade dress, 1988
Although EPS uniforms are becoming more conventional, they still exhibit 'revolutionary simplicity'. Cuban-inspired olive green fatigue shirt, trousers and a 'Castro cap' without insignia serve as field and service uniform for all ranks. On parade white gloves are worn, with Soviet M40 or M60 or Bulgarian M72 helmets, or plain black berets; honour-guards add white gaiters and belts. M1980 officers' shoulder strap rank insignia was in silver: the top two ranks, primarily political, are *Comandante de la Revolución*—a star, with a white embroidered star above black (left) and red (right) crossed branches on the collar; and *Comandante Guerrillero* – blank strap, and white star on red (upper) and black (lower) shield edged silver on the collar. Then two stars—*Comandante de Brigada*; one star – *Comandante*; four chevrons points down – *Subcomandante*; three—*Capitán*; two—*Teniente Primero*; one—*Teniente*; one bar—*Subteniente*. Enlisted ranks wore yellow US-style chevrons on upper sleeves: three chevrons, three bars—*Sargento Primero*; three chevrons, two bars—*Sargento Segundo*; two chevrons, one bar—*Sargento Tercero*; one chevron, one bar—*Soldado de Primera*; no insignia—*Soldado*. On 22 August 1986 new ranks were introduced for ranks above *Capitán*, retaining the two political ranks. Generals wear silver stars above crossed silver sword and branch on shoulder-loops: four stars—*General de Ejercitó* (Humberto Ortega Saavedra, Minister of Defence, Armed Forces Commander); three—*General de Cuerpo*; two—*General de División*; one—*General de Brigada*. Field officers have silver stars: three—

Coronel; two—*Teniente Coronel*; one—*Mayor*. An olive green bush-jacket can now be worn by generals; also subdued EPS and name tapes, and a metal beret badge, but so far no branch or unit insignia.

F4: Nicaragua: Sargento Tercero, 'Simón Bolívar' Irregular Warfare Battalion; combat dress, 1988
In combat élite units such as the BLI's wear a camouflage smock or shirt and trousers, in a variety of patterns of which this seems the most common, with officers' silver rank insignia on the collars, and NCOs' chevrons on upper sleeves. The usual headgear is the Soviet tropical field hat, usually with chin strap pulled tight over the crown—BLIs wear this at all times as a regimental distinction, but US-style baseball caps and camouflaged 'Castro caps' are also worn. This soldier, possibly a party member, wears unofficially a neck scarf in the traditional arnarchist, also now Sandinista, colours of red ('freedom') and black ('or death!'). He has Chinese-pattern chest-pouch webbing with magazines for his Soviet 7.62 mm AKM assault rifle, and grenades

G1: Nicaragua: Guerrilla, Nicaraguan Democratic Front, Quilali Regional Command; combat dress, 1984
None of the six Contra groups has a standardised uniform. They wear civilian clothes, captured Sandinista Army or Militia uniforms, or US-supplied olive green or camouflaged items, in various combinations. In 1982 the FDN achieved a measure of uniformity through large supplies of very dark bluish-green baseball caps, fatigue shirts, jackets and trousers, as shown here. The FDN uses positional titles rather than ranks: *Comandante de Región* (regional commander); *Comandante* (detachment, group or task-force commander); *Jefe de Compania* (company CO); *Jefe de Pelotón* (platoon CO); *Jefe de Escuadra* (squad CO), but no rank insignia. This guerrilla wears a flag-pin badge also worn by ARDE, and the FDN arm badge, both common but not universal insignia. He wears US webbing and carries an M60 machine gun.

G2: Nicaragua: Guerrilla, FDN Special Forces; combat dress, 1988
Standing smartly to attention, this member of the

élite *Comando de Operaciones Especiales* (COE) is identified by the skull badge on his left sleeve. He is wearing captured Sandinista Militia fatigues with the newest national-flag arm badge; a camouflaged 'boonie hat' with unofficial subdued national tab; and US-supplied ALICE webbing and tropical boots. His weapon is a Chinese copy of the Soviet AKM assault rifle, the Type 56/1.

G3: Nicaragua: Guerrilla, Revolutionary Democratic Alliance; combat dress, 1985

Many ARDE members favoured the green beret, for its élite associations, to which this guerrilla has attached a curious home-made triangular cap badge. Wearing one of a wide range of camouflage fatigues (other leaf patterns and tiger-stripes are also encountered), he carries a Rumanian version of the Soviet AKM assault rifle. His national breast-badge is also worn by FDN guerrillas and, like the FDN, ARDE uses positional titles up to and including *Comandante*. As true disciples of Sandino, some ARDE troops still wore the red and black FSLN neck scarf.

H1: Costa Rica: Teniente, Northern Border Security Battalion; combat dress, 1988

Easily mistaken initially for US troops, the field uniform of the *Guardia Civil* is a mixture of US-supplied OG107s, M1967 jungle fatigues, and 'woodland' camouflage shirts and trousers of similar pattern but different cut to US issue. Headgear consists of the M1964 baseball cap, the 'boonie hat', and the M1 helmet. ALICE webbing is worn, and small arms include both M16s and more obsolete types—M1 Garands, and the elderly but excellent Beretta MAB38/49 sub-machine gun depicted.

Above the left breast pocket is worn the 'C.R. Guardia Civil' patch; company patches are seen on the right upper arm. The 1st and 2nd Companies were formed into a battalion to guard the Nicaraguan border, and after serious clashes with Sandinistas in hot pursuit of ARDE guerrillas this became in May 1985 the Northern Border Security Battalion, whose yellow-on-black 'BINICIO' title is seen here on the right shoulder. The brassard indicates *Comando del Norte*, 'Northern Command'. Officers wear standard US Army gold and silver rank insignia on the headgear and right collar, and

US Army branch insignia on the left collar. Enlisted ranks wear yellow-on-green US M1958 chevrons on both sleeves: three chevrons, one rocker—*Sargento*; two chevrons—*Cabo*; one chevron—*Raso primera clase*; none—*Raso*.

H2: Panama: Subteniente, 7th 'Macho de Monte' Fusilier Company, Panama Defence Forces; combat dress, 1988

Defence Forces officers wear US M1957 green service dress, with peaked cap with gold national crest, gold wire chin strap and peak embroidery for field and general officers, green jacket and trousers. The khaki equivalent uniform is also worn. The brass national title 'RP' (Republicá de Panama) appears on the jacket collar, and on the lapel the branch badge: star in a wreath—generals and General Staff; crossed rifles—infantry. Officers' brass rank insignia is worn on the shoulder straps (or green shoulder loops on shirts), but generals and General Staff always wear stiff green shoulder boards edged gold: national crest above four five-pointed stars – *General de Brigada* (FD Commander Manuel Antonio Noriega); three stars only—*Coronel*; two—*Teniente Coronel*; one—*Mayor*; three horizontal linked bars—*Capitán*; two—*Teniente*; one—*Subteniente*. Enlisted ranks wear US-style M1958 yellow chevrons on green on OG107 fatigue shirt upper sleeves: three chevrons, one rocker—*Sargento de Primera*; three chevrons—*Sargento de Segunda*; two—*Cabo*; no insignia—*Soldado Raso*.

The M1 helmet or US peaked field cap is worn in the field, with OG107 shirt and trousers or olive jungle utilities, currently being replaced by the US BDU camouflage clothing already worn by the élite 7th Company. Officers wear brass rank badges on the right collar, branch insignia on the left, company title on upper sleeves, and parachute wings above the left pocket. He wears US ALICE webbing, and carries an UZI sub-machine gun.

H3: Haiti: Sergent-Fourrier, Presidential Guard, Haitian Army; parade uniform, 1988

More common than the dark blue officers' ceremonial uniform is the US M1957 khaki service dress with black tie. The peaked cap has a gold braid chin strap, brass national crest on a trophy of cannons as cap badge, laurel branches on the peak for field officers and generals, and laurel encircling the dark blue cap band for generals. The jacket collar carries the brass title 'RD'H' (République d'Haiti), the lapel brass branch insignia: star—General Staff; crossed rifles—infantry. Generals' shoulder strap rank insignia consists of three large vertically placed silver stars: three—*Lieutenant Général*; two—*Général de Division*; one—*Général de Brigade*; field officers, small vertical brass stars: three—*Colonel*; two—*Lieutenant Colonel*; one—*Major*; company officers, brass linked chevrons, point down: three—*Capitaine*; two—*Lieutenant*; one—*Sous-Lieutenant*; one (point up)—*Adjudant* (Warrant Officer). Enlisted ranks wear a khaki garrison cap, M1957 cap (or obsolete M1942 cap) with plain chin strap, shirt, tie and trousers, and US-style yellow chevrons on dark brown backing on upper sleeves: three chevrons, three horizontal bars—*Sergent Major*; three chevrons, hollow rhomboid—*Sergent Premier*; three chevrons, one bar—*Sergent Fourrier*; three chevrons—*Sergent*; two *Caporal*; one—*Soldat de première classe*; none—*Soldat*. This uniform with M1 helmet doubles as field dress, although OG107 fatigues are also worn, with 'woodland' or 'duck-hunter' pattern camouflage fatigues for Presidential Guard and 'Léopards'. The Guard wears 'GP' (Garde Présidentielle) titles on the collar (above shoulder strap rank insignia, for officers) and a unit shoulder patch. This soldier wears obsolete US 10-pouch webbing, and carries the M1 Garand rifle.

H4: Haiti: Militiaman, National Security Volunteers, 1985
Not to be confused with the plain-clothes 'Tontons Macoutes' political police, the Volunteers, supposedly modelled on Mussolini's MVSN black-

Col. Hugo Torres, political chief of the Sandinista Army in 1987, wearing the new rank insignia introduced in August 1986.

shirt militia, wore ex-Police peaked caps or this distinctive beret, blue shirt and trousers, and red scarves or armbands. Equipped with obsolete weapons such as this M1928A1 Thompson submachine gun, and the M1 Garand, or the Israeli UZI, they were abolished in February 1986 with the departure of 'Baby Doc' Duvalier.

Notes sur les planches en couleur
A1 Uniforme dans le style des US; insigne de col avec numéro et fusils croisés et cordons de casque verts précisent l'infanterie et le régiment. **A2** Les vêtements civils étaient portés par la plupart des guérillos, mais treillis 'surplus' de l'armée des US était préféré par les commandants. Le béret noir révolutionnaire porte l'insigne d'étoile d'un chef de bataillon de l'armée cubaine. Le brassard est celui du mouvement 'Vingtième Juillet' de Castro. **A3** Tenue de cérémonie dans le style soviétique, introduite pendant les années soixante-dix.

B1 Treillis et équipement dans les style soviétique, avec galons jaunes de rang sur l'épaule au-dessus du chiffre *FAR*. Casques soviétiques modèle 1940 et casques bulgares sont portés tous les deux. **B2** Les soldats de cette unité portent des uniformes presque identiques aux uniformes de l'Infanterie de Marine Soviétique; remarquez l'insigne d'unité sur la manche. **B3** Cimier national sur le devant du casque, et insigne des régiments de la garde sur les deux manches. L'insigne de bataillon sur le col se compose d'un soldat avec le cimier national sur fond rouge. L'écharpe, les gants et les lacets de chaussure blancs sont portés pour service de cérémonie. Le fusil est le fusil allemand *G3*.

Farbtafeln
A1 Im amerikanischen Stil gehaltene Uniform; Nummer und gekreuztes Gewehrabzeichen auf dem Kragen. Grüne Mützenkordel weisen auf Infanterie und das Regiment hin. **A2** Die meisten Aufständischen trugen Zivilbekleidung, von den Führern wurden jedoch erbeutete amerikanische Drillichuniformen aus Überschußbeständen bevorzugt. Die schwarze Baskenmütze aus der Revolution birgt die Sterninsignie der kubanischen Armee. Die Armbinde erinnert an Castros '20 Juli Bewegung'. **A3** Eine auf sowjetischem Schnitt beruhende Ausgehuniform, die im Laufe der siebziger Jahre eingeführt wurde.

B1 Im sowjetischen Stil gehaltene Drillichuniform sowie Ausrüstung mit gelben Rangstreifen über den Schulterstreifen über der '*FAR*'—Ziffer. Sowjetische Helme aus dem Jahre 1940 oder bulgarische Helme aus dem Jahr 1972 wurden getragen. **B2** Diese kleine Einheit trägt eine Uniform, die mit der der sowjetische Marineinfanterie nahezu identisch ist. Zu beachten ist die Einheitsinsignie am Ärmel. **B3** Das Nationalwappen ist an der Vorderseite des Helms sowie auf beiden Seiten des Wachabzeichens am Ärmel zu erkennen. Das Kragenabzeichen des Bataillons birgt einen Soldaten und das Nationalwappen

C1 Uniforme de camouflage sud-coréen, avec bérets rouges des *Forces Spéciaux* qui portent l'étiquette *Kaibil* au-dessus de l'insigne de grade miniature. L'équipement se compose d'éléments *US M1956*; les armes portées sont les modèles *Uzi*, *Galil* et *M16*. **C2** Une copie, probablement localement faite, de l'uniforme de camouflage *US Army BDU*, avec équipement *M1967* et mitrailleuse *M60*; l'insigne sur la manche est celui de la Première Zone Militaire. **C3** Tenue de cérémonie verte dans le style *US Army* avec parement modifié pointu; les insignes de grade se trouvent sur les épaulettes, les insignes de section sur le col et les insignes d'unité en métallle sont attachés à la poche; ils sont aussi portés sur l'épaule gauche en forme brodée. Des ailes de parachutiste semblables aux ailes *US* sont portées sur la poitrine gauche.

D1 Uniforme démodé influencé par la *Guardia Civil* d'Espagne. Insigne National sur le côté du casque, insigne *G.N* sur le devant du casque et sur les deux épaules, chiffres *G.N* sur le col, chevrons de grade dans le style de l'armée, et insigne de tireur d'élite sur la poitrine gauche. **D2** Treillis et casque de camouflage *US* avec écharpe bleu clair d'infanterie portée seulement pour les revues; les insignes de grade noirs étaient portés sur le col droit et les insignes de section sur le col gauche avec tenue de corvée; les insignes d'unité sont quelquefois portés sur les deux épaules. **D3** Camouflage 'bois' *US* et camouflage 'vague' sud-coréen sont portés tous les deux. Au champ de bataille les insignes—comme par exemple l'étiquette *Cazador* et les insignes de grade—sont ôtés du béret noir. Équipement *US* de plusieurs sortes est en usage. **D4** Les marines utilisent le béret noir *Cazador* avec leur propre insigne d'unité, qui est utilisé en forme adoucie sur le col.

E1 La plupart des soldats portent un treillis *US* vert olive, mais cet officier parachutiste a une chemise curieusement façonnée en étoffe de camouflage *BDU* et un béret assorti qui porte son insigne de grade et ses ailes sur un fond losange rouge qui indique sa section. Remarquez les insignes d'armée sur les manches en couleurs douces, l'équipement *ALICE* et le casque israélien avec couverture camouflée différente. **E2** Uniforme et béret de camouflage 'chasseur de canard' avec insigne d'armée en plein couleurs sur la manche et insigne d'unité sur le bras gauche; les étiquettes *Ranger* (US) at *Teson* (Honduras) sont portées sur l'épaule gauche. **E3** Camouflage *US* modifié avec poches noires, épaulettes noires et calot noir. Insigne de bataillon sur l'épaule gauche et mitraillette *CAR15*.

F1 Treillis de jungle *US* avec chevrons de grade dans le style *US*, casque israélien, fusil *Galil* et insigne d'unité sur l'épaule. Il y a un ruban de noms tissés sur la poitrine droite et un titre national sur la gauche qui sont cachés par les cartouchières. **F2** Eden Pastora, la 'Comandante Zero', en costume caractéristique. **F3** Uniforme dans le style cubain avec insignes de grade simples sur les épaulettes et rubans de noms tissés et de titre national sur la poitrine; il n'y a pas d'insigne de section ou d'unité. **F4** Il paraît que ce dessin de camouflage était le plus fréquent. Il est porté ici avec la casque colonial, qui est une particularité portée avec fierté par les Bataillons de Guerre Irrégulière, ou *BLIs*. Équipement dans le style chinois et écharpe Sandiniste en couleurs anarchiste.

G1 Les guérillos *FDN* ont recevu une quantité de ces vêtements bleu-verts très foncé en 1982. L'insigne sur le calot est aussi porté par les soldats *ARDE*, mais l'insigne sur le bras est particulier aux soldats *FDN*. **G2** Uniforme kaki saisi de la Milice Sandiniste, calot de camouflage dans le style *US* avec titre national, pièce en forme de drapeau national sur la manche et, sur le bras gauche, insigne 'tête de mort' des *Forces Spéciaux* Contra, ou *COE*. La mélange d'équipement est caractéristique. **G3** Les soldats *ARDE* préfèrent le béret vert, ici avec l'insigne *ARDE*. L'uniforme est une copie du treillis *US*, et la mitrailleuse est le modèle roumain de la mitrailleuse *AK*. Quelques guérillos *ARDE* portent toujours l'écharpe rouge et noire, et prétendent maintenir l'esprit vrai des premiers Sandinistes. L'insigne sur la poitrine est aussi porté par les soldats *FDN*.

H1 Les soldats portaient une variété de styles *US*, comme par exemple cette mélange de treillis de jungle et d'uniformes *OG107*. Équipement *ALICE* est toujours utilisé; quelques mitraillettes *Beretta* sont toujours utilisées côté à côté avec les mitraillettes *M16*. Insignes de grade sur le casque et sur le col droit, insignes *Guardia Civil* sur la poitrine gauche. Le titre du bataillon '*Binicio*' est porté sur l'épaule droite; le brassard indique le Commandement du Nord. **H2** Cette unité d'élite est la première avec uniforme de camouflage *BDU*, qui commence maintenant à remplacer le treillis olive. Remarquez le béret, l'insigne et les titres d'épaule d'unité, et les insignes de grade et de section *US* sur le col. **H3** Uniformes et équipement *US* démodés, avec chiffre en cuivre *GP* sur le col et insigne *Garde Présidentielle* sur l'épaule. **H4** Les volontaires portaient des anciens képis de police ou par exemple ce béret singulier, avec des chemises et des pantalons bleus et une écharpe touge attachée quelquepart sur le corps ou sur l'arme. Les armes étaient une mélange de modèles modernes et démodés.

---

auf einem roten Hintergrund. Weißer Schal, Handschuhe und Schnursenkel wurden zu offiziellen Anlässen getragen. Beim Gewehr handelt es sich um ein deutsches G3.

C1 Der südkoreanische Tarnanzug wurde mit der roten Baskenmütze der Spezialeinheiten getragen. An der Mütze war der '*Kaibil*'—Qualifikationsstreifen über der verkleinerten Ranginsignie angebracht. Die Ausrüstung entspricht dem *US M1956* Muster. Zur Bewaffnung zählen die *Uzi*, *Galil* und *M16*. **C2** Hierbei handelt es sich wahrscheinlich um eine regionale Kopie der US ARMY BDU Tarnuniform mit *M1967* Austrüstung sowie M60 Maschinengewehr. Das Armabzeichen ist von der 1 Militärzone. **C3** Diese im amerikanischen Stil gehaltene grüne Ausgehuniform besitzt veränderte, spitz zu laufende Ärmelaufschläge. Rangabzeichen befinden sich auf den Schulterstreifen, Abteilungsabzeichen sind an Kragen ersichtlich. Das metallene Einheitsabzeichen ist an der Tasche befestigt und wird in verzierter From auf der linken Schulter getragen. Die Fallschirmspringer flügel ähneln dem amerikanischen Muster und werden auf der linken Brusthälfte getragen.

D1 Eine altmodische Uniform, die durch die spanische *Guardia Civil* beeinflußt wurde. Das Nationalwappen ist auf der Seite des Helms ersichtlich, und das *GN*-Abzeichen wird an der Vorderseite getragen. Darüber hinaus werden *GN*-Abzeichen auf beiden Schultern, und *G.N*-Ziffern an Kragen getragen. **D2** Amerikanische Drillichuniform mit Helm, hellblauem Infanterieschal für Paraden. Auf der Drillichuniform sind schwarze Ranginsignien auf dem rechten Kragen, und Abteilungsabzeichen auf dem linken Kragen ersichtlich. Einheitsinsignien werden manchmal auf beiden Schultern getragen. **D3** Die im amerikanischen Stil gehaltene 'Woodland' und südkoreanische 'Wave' Tarnuniform wurden getragen. Im Feld bzw. z.B. der '*Cazador*'-Streifen und die Ranginsignie—die Insignien an der Baskenmütze. Autrüstung verschiedener amerikanischer Muster wird verwendet. **D4** Die Marine benutzt die schwarze Baskenmütze der *Cazadores* zusammen mit dem Einheitsabzeichen, welches in einter unauffälligeren Abwandlung auf der Schulter nochmals wiederholt ist.

E1 Die meisten Soldaten tragen die amerikanische oliv-grüne Drillichuniform. Dieser Fallschirmjäger besitzt jedoch ein eigenartig geschnittenes Hemd, das im *BDU*-Tarnanzugstil gehalten ist, sowie die passende Baskenmütze mit seinem Rang und den Fallschirmflügeln auf einer Raute in roter Abteilungsfarbe. Zu beachten ist die Ärmelinsignie in weniger auffallenden Farben, die *ALICE* Austrüstung und der israelische Helm mit unterschiedlichen Tarnüberzügen. **E2** Der 'Duck-Hunter'-Tarnanzug mit Baskenmütze mit der vollständigen Ärmelinsignie und Einheitsinsignie auf der linken Brusthälfte. Aus den USA und Honduras stammende '*Ranger*' und '*Teson*' Qualifikationsstreifen werden auf der linken Schulter getragen. **E3** Veränderter amerikanischer Tarnanzug mit schwarz gefärbten Taschen und zusätzlichen schwarzen Schulterstreifen und Mütze. Die Bataillonsinsignie ist auf der linken Schulter. *CAR15* Maschinenpistole.

F1 Amerikanische Dschungeldrillichuniform mit im amerikanischen Stil gehaltenen Winkelrangabzeichen, israelischem Helm un *Galil*-Gewehr und Einheitsschulterinsignie. Hinter dem Patronengurt befindet sich der Namenstreifen auf der rechten Brusthälfte und das Nationalabzeichen links. **F2** Eden Pastora, 'Comandante Zero', in typischer Bekleidung. **F3** Eine im kubanischen Stil gehaltene Uniform mit einfachen ranginsignien auf den Schulterstreifen, Name und Nationalabzeichen auf der Brust. Eine Abteilungs- oder Einheitsinsignie existiert nicht. **F4** Von den verschiedenen Tarnmustern scheinbar das am häufigsten benutzte. Hier mit der im sowjetischen Stil gehaltenen Buschmütze, die einen prächtigen Unterschied der 'Irregular Warfare Battalions' (*BLI*) bildet. Austrüstung ist im chinesischen Stil gehalten. Dazu gehört auch der Sandinista Schal in den Anarchistenfarben.

G1 1982 erhielten die *FDN*-Aufständischen Lieferungen dieser sehr dunklen blau-grünen Uniform. Das Mützenabzeichen wurde auch von den *ARDE* getragen. Das Armabzeichen wurde nur von der *FDN* verwendet. **G2** Erbeutete Khakiuniform der sandinistischen Miliz. Der im amerikanischen Stil gehaltene Tarnhut birgt das Nationalwappen. Die Nationalfahne befindet sich auf der Ärmelabzeichen. Links ist der Totenkopf der Contra 'Spezialeinheiten', der *COE*, angebracht. Die Mischung verschiedener Austrüstung ist typisch. **G3** Die *ARDE* bevorzugt die grünen Baskenmützen, die hier mit dem *ARDE*-Mützenabzeichen getragen werden. Die Uniform beruht auf einer Kopie der amerikanischen Drillichuniform. Die Waffe ist eine rumänische Version der *AK*. Einige der *ARDE*-Aufständischen trugen immer noch den roten und schwarzen Schal, da sie behaupten, daß damit die wirkliche Gesinnung der ursprünglichen Sandinistas weitergeführt wird. Das Brustabzeichen wird ebenso von der *FDN* getragen.

H1 Verschiedene Uniformen wurden getragen. Hier eine MIschung aus '*OG107*' und Dschungeldrillichuniformen. *ALICE* Tarnnetzausrüstung wurde verwendet. Neben den *M16* wurden auch noch einige *Beretta* Maschinenpistolen eingesetzt. Die Ranginsignien befinden sich auf der Mütze und dem rechten Kragen, Infanterieabteilungsinsignien links und *Guardia Civil* Insignien auf der linken Brusthälfte. Das Bataillonsabzeichen '*Binicio*' wird auf der rechten Schulter getragen. Die Armbinde weist auf den 'Northern Command' (Nordkommando) hin. **H2** Diese Eliteeinheit ist die erst mit *BDU*-Tarnunfirom, die nunmehr die olivfarbenen Tarnanzüge ersetzt. Zu beachten ist die Baskenmütze der Einheit, das Einheitsabzeichen, die Schulterabzeichen, die amerikanischen Krageninsignien des Rangs und der Abteilung. **H3** Veraltete amerikanische Uniformen und Austrüstungen, mit messingfarbener '*GP*' Krageneziffer und 'Presidential Guard' Schulterinsignie. **H4** Freiwillige trugen ehemalige Polizistenmütze oder diese ungewöhnliche Baskenmütze, blaue Hemden und Hosen und einen roten Schal um den Körper oder die Waffe gebunden. Die Bewaffnung setzte sich aus einer Mischung von veralteten und modernen Waffengattungen zusammen.